PATRICK M(

ASTRONOMY
—★QUIZ BOOK★—

GEORGE PHILIP

British Library Cataloguing in Publication Data

Moore, Patrick
  Patrick Moore's astronomy quiz book.
  1. Astronomy—Miscellanea
  I. Title
  520'.76   QB44.2

ISBN 0-540-01160-6

©Patrick Moore 1987

Illustrations © Paul Doherty 1987

Published by George Philip & Son Ltd
27A Floral Street, London WC2E 9DP

Filmset by Tameside Filmsetting Ltd,
Ashton-under-Lyne, Lancashire
Printed by BAS Printers Ltd,
Over Wallop, Hampshire
Bound by Robert Hartnoll Ltd,
Bodmin, Cornwall

CONTENTS

FOREWORD

This Quiz Book can be used in many different
ways. I have begun with two very simple sets of
questions, followed by quizzes on specialized
branches of astronomy and then five General
Knowledge sections, which become increasingly
difficult. Quiz 18 is decidedly light-hearted, and the
last two are, to be candid, obscure!

One alternative method is to make up quizzes by
taking, say, all the No. 1 questions from the
different sections, and so on; there is scope for
many permutations.

There are quite a number of questions in which
you are invited to select the 'odd one out'. For
example, suppose that we were having a
geography quiz, and you were asked to select the
'odd one out' from Greece, Finland, France,
Uruguay and Austria; the answer would be
Uruguay, because Uruguay is in South America
whereas all the rest are in Europe.

Well – I hope you enjoy testing yourselves and
others!

Patrick Moore
Selsey, 1987

THE QUESTIONS

QUIZ
1

Fundamentals

1 What is the difference between a planet and a star?
2 How long does it take the Earth to spin round once on its axis?
3 How long does it take the Earth to go once round the Sun?
4 What is an orbit?
5 If you go to Australia, will you see the same stars as you do from England?

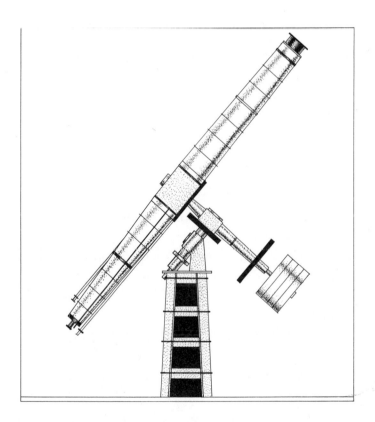

6 So far, have we ever sent an unmanned spacecraft to any planet?
7 Can we ever see the Moon in the daytime?
8 Does light travel at a definite speed? If so, what?
9 Why does the Sun rise toward the east and set toward the west?
10 Name the 'odd one out': Mars, Jupiter, Saturn, Sirius, Venus.

True or False?

1 Greenwich Observatory is Britain's leading astrological institution.
2 The Moon shines by reflecting the light of the Sun.
3 All stars are suns.
4 There is no gravity above the top of the atmosphere.
5 The Sun is the central body of the universe.
6 A comet moves across the sky in less than five minutes.
7 The Moon can sometimes pass in front of high clouds.
8 The sky looks blue because the Earth's air scatters the blue part of the Sun's light.
9 The Earth is closer to the Sun in January than in June.
10 A planet seems to wander slowly about from one star-group to another.

QUIZ 2

More fundamentals

1 What is a satellite, and how many natural satellites has the Earth?
2 What is the most important body in the Solar System?
3 What is a constellation?
4 What star seems to stay almost motionless in the sky as seen from northern latitudes? Can this star be seen from New Zealand?
5 What is meant by escape velocity, and what is its value in the case of the Earth?
6 Are the stars closer to us or further away than the planets?
7 Is there atmosphere all the way between the Earth and the Moon?
8 What is the Galaxy?
9 Is the age of the Earth (a) about 10,000 years (b) about 4700 thousand million years (c) about a million million years (d) about 6000 years?
10 Will the year 2000 be a leap year?

True or False?

1 The Moon has a very well-marked effect upon the weather.
2 The largest planets are Venus, Mars and Pluto.
3 At the South Pole, there is six months' day followed by six months' night.
4 All the stars move round the Sun.

5 It is dangerous to look straight at the Sun through binoculars.
6 Artificial satellites are closer to us than the Moon.
7 From the bottom of a deep well, you can see stars in the daytime.
8 Men have been to the Moon and Mars.
9 A shooting-star is a star which has been dislodged from its usual position in the sky.
10 In July, daylight lasts for longer in Iceland than in Spain.

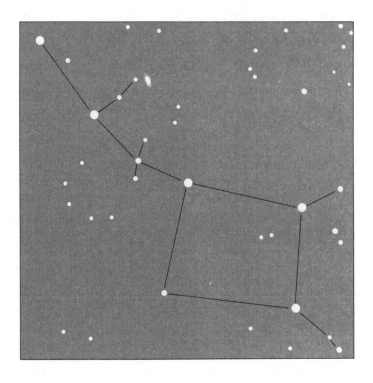

QUIZ
3

History

1 Who was the last great astronomer of ancient times, after whom the Ptolemaic System was named?

2 In 1543 a Polish astronomer published a book in which he claimed that the Earth moves round the Sun. Who was he?

3 Who wrote the *Principia*?

4 Who was the first man to go into space, and when?

5 Name the 'odd one out': Hubble, Ryle, Hale, Shapley, Curtis.

6 Who was the first great astronomer to use a telescope?

7 Who first described the principle of the reflecting telescope?

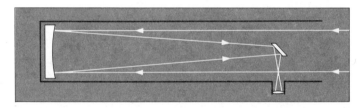

8 Who measured the distance of the star 61 Cygni, in 1838?

9 Give the Christian names of the following astronomers: Brahe, Eddington, Spencer Jones, Hoyle, Flammarion.

10 Name the famous German rocket scientist who was largely responsible for developing the V2 rocket weapon, and later played the major rôle in launching America's first artificial satellite.

True or False?

1 The first telescope whose existence can be proved was made by a Dutch spectacle-maker, Hans Lippershey, in about 1608.

2 Sir Christopher Wren was a professional astronomer.

3 Only one woman has ever become Astronomer Royal of Britain.

4 A famous Danish astronomer kept a pet dwarf, had a false nose, and equipped his observatory with a prison.

5 The theory of relativity was first developed by Albert Epstein.

6 Johannes Kepler published the first of his Laws of Planetary Motion in the year 1709.

7 Charles Conrad was the second man to step on to the surface of the Moon.

8 The Romans were the first to divide up the stars into constellation patterns.

9 The Egyptians used to measure their seasons by observing the heliacal rising of Sirius (that is to say, the date when in each year Sirius could first be observed in the dawn sky).

10 Minor Planet No. 518 is named after a cake.

QUIZ
4

Instruments

1 What is meant by an equatorial mounting for a telescope?
2 What is the INT, and where is it?
3 Where is the world's largest refracting telescope?
4 In which English county is the famous Jodrell Bank radio telescope?
5 Which telescope was nicknamed 'the Leviathan of Parsonstown'?
6 On which volcano would you find UKIRT?
7 The UHURU satellite, launched in 1971, carried a special type of telescope. What was this telescope designed to study?
8 In which century was the Royal Greenwich Observatory founded – and why?
9 What makes the Hubble Telescope so exceptional?
10 In which country are the observatories of La Silla, Las Campanas and Cerro Tololo?

True or False?

1 An instrument used to split up a beam of light and spread it out into a rainbow is called an interferometer.
2 A transit instrument can swing only in an east–west direction.
3 The official name of the Palomar 200-inch (508-centimetre) reflector is the Lick Telescope.

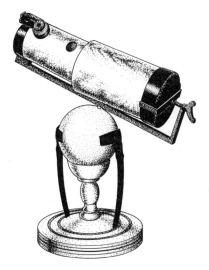

4 The mirror for a large telescope at the Paris Observatory was made from the porthole of a dismantled battleship.

5 The world's largest single-mirror telescope is at Mount Semirodriki, in the USSR.

6 The world's highest major observatory is at Boulder, Colorado.

7 The first modern-type planetarium was designed by Dr W. Bauersfeld of the Zeiss Optical Works in Germany.

8 The Helwan Observatory is in Saudi Arabia.

9 The Mount Wilson Hooker telescope has been closed because of light pollution from the city of Los Angeles.

10 If you have a pair of 7 × 50 binoculars, it means that each main lens is 7 centimetres in diameter and that the magnifying power is 50.

QUIZ
5

The Sun

1 What is the approximate distance between the Sun and the Earth?
2 Why does a sunspot look dark?
3 What are the Fraunhofer lines, and why are they so called?
4 Is the Sun burning in the same way as a coal fire?
5 How long does the Sun take to complete one journey round the centre of the Galaxy?
6 What are the three types of solar eclipses, and what is the difference between them?
7 What is the solar photosphere?
8 When does the Sun reach its northernmost point in the sky every year?

9 What is the spectral type of the Sun?
10 What is the solar cycle, and what is its approximate length?

True or False?

1 The Sun is much less luminous than the Pole Star.
2 The last total solar eclipse visible in England was that of 1954.
3 The distance between the Sun and the Earth was formerly measured by observations of the planet Saturn.
4 Auroræ or polar lights are caused by electrified particles sent out by the Sun.
5 The Sun is losing mass at the rate of 4000 tons per second.
6 The temperature of the Sun is 18,000°F (10,000°C) at its surface and about 90,000°F (50,000°C) at its centre.
7 The solar wind is the name given to the monsoon over North Africa and the Atlantic Ocean.
8 American scientists are studying the Sun from an observatory in a gold-mine a mile below ground.
9 A total solar eclipse can happen only at the time of full moon.
10 The Sun's volume is over a million times that of the Earth.

The Moon

1 To the nearest day, how long does the Moon take to complete one journey round the Earth – or, more precisely, round the centre of gravity of the Earth–Moon system?
2 How is a lunar eclipse caused?
3 Why does part of the Moon's surface always stay turned away from the Earth?
4 Has the Moon any atmosphere? If not, why not?
5 In which lunar 'sea' did *Apollo 11* land in July 1969?
6 What is an occultation – and why are lunar occultations useful to astronomers?
7 Name the 'odd one out': Tycho, Copernicus, Descartes, Pico, Schickard, Theophilus.
8 Give the English names for: Sinus Iridum, Mare Nubium, Lacus Mortis, Mare Frigoris, Oceanus Procellarum.
9 What is the lunar regolith?
10 To date, who was the last man to walk on the Moon's surface, and when?

True or False?

1 The Moon is the largest satellite in the Solar System.
2 The deepest of all the lunar craters is named Hell.
3 The first spacecraft to send back pictures of the Moon's far side was *Luna 3*, in 1959.

4 The Moon's magnetic field is half as strong as that of the Earth.

5 The Soviet Mountains, rising to 20,000 feet (6000 metres), run across the far side of the Moon only.

6 When low down, the full moon is larger in the sky than when it is higher up.

7 On the Moon, the sky is always black even at lunar noon.

8 Lunar craters have been named after Julius Cæsar, Winston Churchill, Vasco da Gama, Neil Armstrong and H. G. Wells.

9 Barycentre is the largest of all the Moon's walled plains.

10 A new large lunar crater, in the Mare Crisium, was formed in September 1879.

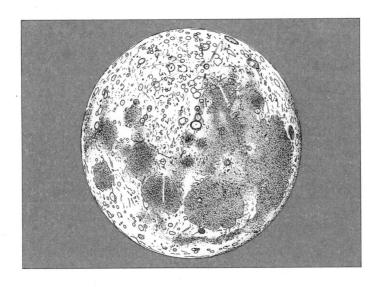

The planets

1 Name the planets, in order of distance from the Sun in 1988.
2 Which planet can come closest to the Earth?
3 Which is the only planet known to have canals on its surface?
4 Which planets show phases from new to full, like those of the Moon?
5 On which planet would you find Olympus Mons, Syrtis Major and Valles Marineris?
6 Name the four largest satellites of Jupiter.
7 Give the 'odd one out': Rhea, Deimos, Iris, Enceladus, Nereid, Tethys.
8 Which planet has the shortest day, and, to the nearest hour, what is its length?
9 Which is (a) the largest of the nine planets, (b) the smallest of the nine planets, (c) the planet bypassed by *Voyager 2* in January 1986, (d) the planet with the strongest magnetic field, (e) the planet discovered by William Herschel in 1781?

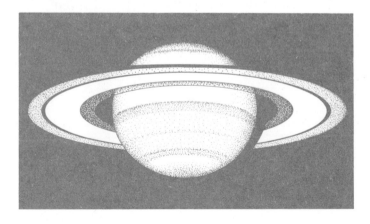

10 The first four asteroids were discovered between 1800 and 1810. Name them.

True or False?

1 Mercury always keeps the same face turned toward the Sun.
2 The main gap in Saturn's ring system is known as the Cassini Division.
3 The dark markings on the surface of Mars were first reported by the Norwegian astronomer Vastitas Borealis in 1659.
4 The asteroid belt lies between the orbits of Jupiter and Saturn.
5 Uranus and Neptune are just visible with the naked eye if you know where to look for them.
6 Asteroids have been named after Clyde Tombaugh and Patrick Moore.
7 The *Voyager 1* spacecraft will return to the neighbourhood of the Earth about the year 2061.
8 Nobody now living can remember seeing a transit of Venus.
9 The ground pressure of the Martian atmosphere is about the same as that of the Earth's atmosphere on the summit of Mount Everest.
10 The first spacecraft to bypass Jupiter was *Pioneer 10*, in 1973.

Comets and meteoroids

1 Does a comet's tail point (a) toward the Sun, (b) away from the Sun, (c) sideways?
2 Halley's Comet last came back in 1986. What were the dates of its last two previous returns?
3 Do all comets have tails?
4 Who discovered (a) Faye's Comet, (b) Encke's Comet, (c) D'Arrest's Comet?
5 What exactly is a meteor radiant?
6 In which months do the following meteor showers occur: (a) the Quadrantids, (b) the Perseids, (c) the Leonids.
7 Name the brilliant comet of 1858, usually said to be the most beautiful ever seen.
8 Where is Meteor Crater?
9 What is a sporadic meteor?
10 What is, or is believed to be, the Oort Cloud?

True or False?

1 The average shooting-star meteor is about one inch in diameter.
2 Meteorites usually fall during violent thunderstorms.
3 The brightest comet of the twentieth century, so far, has been Kohoutek's Comet of 1973.
4 The heads of some comets are larger than the Earth.
5 The Star of Bethlehem is now believed to have been Halley's Comet.
6 The largest known meteorite is still lying where it fell in Southern Africa; it weighs at least 60 tons.
7 The Leonid meteors were exceptionally rich in 1866, 1933 and 1966.
8 An aerolite is a meteorite which is formed from frozen water in the Earth's upper atmosphere.
9 Encke's Comet has the shortest known period (3.3 years).
10 During the past 500 years, three people have been killed by falling meteorites.

Stars and constellations

1 What is the Latin name for the constellation whose seven main stars make up the pattern often called the Plough or the Big Dipper?

2 What bright star is almost overhead from England during winter evenings?

3 On a summer evening in Scotland, where would you see Orion?

4 Give the 'odd one out': Aries, Libra, Pisces, Cygnus, Taurus, Aquarius.

5 Arrange the following stars in order of apparent brilliancy: Polaris, Alpha Centauri, Rigel, Canopus, Deneb.

6 Give the English names of the following constellations: Microscopium, Canes Venatici, Monoceros, Aquila, Lacerta.

7 Identify the stars often called (a) the Eye of the Bull, (b) the Dog Star, (c) the Wonderful Star, (d) the Garnet Star, (e) the Solitary one.

8 Which star was the north pole star when the Pyramids were built? Why is it no longer the pole star?

9 Give the proper names of (a) Alpha Leonis, (b) Eta Tauri, (c) Zeta Ursæ Majoris, (d) Alpha Scorpii, (e) Alpha Geminorum.

10 Can you see Canopus from (a) London, (b) Athens, (c) Cairo, (d) Sydney, (e) Auckland?

True or False?

1 The planet Saturn is always to be found in Taurus, Cancer or Gemini.

2 The Southern Cross is the smallest constellation in the sky.

3 The brightest star in any constellation is always given the Greek letter Alpha.

4 From Gibraltar, you can just see the Southern Cross.

5 The only bright star with a strongly green colour is Vega.

6 Virgo was a Roman astronomer, after whom the constellation is named.

7 Capricornus is officially the tenth constellation of the Zodiac.

8 The two brightest stars in Orion are Betelgeux and Procyon.

9 In the constellation of the Scorpion there are three first-magnitude stars.

10 The constellation of Cancer (the Crab) lies between Leo and Gemini.

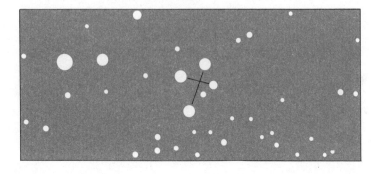

QUIZ
10

The stars: special

1 What is a binary star?
2 What is the HR Diagram, and who devised it?
3 Why is Barnard's Star, 6 light-years away, often known as the Runaway Star?
4 Classify the following variable stars: (a) Eta Aquilæ, (b) U Orionis, (c) Chi Cygni, (d) Delta Libræ, (e) Zeta Geminorum.
5 Explain the term 'absolute magnitude'.
6 What is the significance of the mnemonic 'O Be A Fine Girl Kiss Me Right Now Sweetie'?
7 A nova which flared up in 1918 became temporarily brighter than any star in the sky apart from Sirius. In which constellation was it – and can it still be seen?
8 What is the difference between Type I and Type II supernovæ?
9 What is (a) a Wolf-Rayet star, (b) a Brown Dwarf, (c) a dwarf nova?
10 In 1960, radio astronomers tried to detect intelligent signals from the stars Tau Ceti and Epsilon Eridani. Why were these particular stars selected?

True or False?

1 You can see about 3,000,000 stars with the naked eye on a really clear night.
2 During the past 5000 years, the star Hamal has moved from the constellation Taurus into Aries.

3 In 1840 the three brightest stars in the sky were Sirius, Canopus and Eta Carinæ.

4 Sirius is approaching us so rapidly that in 10,000 years' time it will be bright enough to be seen in daylight.

5 The variations of Algol were first explained by a blind astronomer, Goodricke, in 1783.

6 The brightest supernova of the past thousand years flared up in Lupus (the Wolf) in 1006.

7 Stars of spectral type A are orange-yellow in colour.

8 In 1983 the stars Vega and Fomalhaut, among others, were found to be associated with cool material from which planets may be formed.

9 The Companion of Sirius was discovered at the Mount Wilson Observatory in 1915 by W. S. Adams.

10 Of the stars within ten light-years of the Sun, only Sirius and Alpha Centauri are visible with the naked eye.

QUIZ
11

The Milky Way

1 What is the difference between a globular cluster and a galaxy?

2 What is the popular nickname for the star-cluster known officially as the Pleiades – and why?

3 In which constellation is Præsepe – and can you see it with the naked eye?

4 Many clusters and nebulæ are known by their M or Messier numbers. What are the popular names of M.57, M.97, M.27, M.8 and M.45?

5 What is the Coal Sack, and where would you find it?

6 In 1054 a brilliant supernova flared up in Taurus. What is the name of its remnant which we can see today?

7 Where is the Horse's Head Nebula?

8 Give the 'odd one out': the Wild Duck, the Jewel Box, Omega Centauri, the Sword-Handle in Perseus.

9 Who made the first reasonably good measurement of the size of the Galaxy?

10 How far is the Sun from the centre of the Galaxy: (a) less then 10,000 light-years, (b) less than 20,000 light-years, (c) less than 50,000 light-years?

True or False?

1 The Milky Way is made up of millions of planets, all moving round the centre of the system.

2 The Hercules Globular is the brightest globular cluster in the northern hemisphere of the sky, and was discovered by Edmond Halley.

3 A pulsar is a very small stellar remnant made up of neutrons, spinning round very rapidly.

4 Radio waves from the Milky Way were first detected by Karl Jansky in 1931.

5 All planetary nebulæ are expanding.

6 In the centre of a globular cluster, the average distance between stars is about 10,000,000 miles (16,000,000 kilometres).

7 Our Galaxy is spiral in form, with an overall diameter of approximately 100,000 light-years.

8 The Hyades star-cluster is made up of a v-formation of faint stars extending from Arcturus.

9 The centre of the Galaxy lies in the direction of the star-clouds in Cygnus.

10 A cupful of neutron star material would weigh about a thousand tons.

QUIZ
12

The Universe

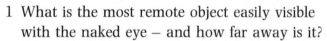

1 What is the most remote object easily visible with the naked eye – and how far away is it?

2 The two brightest external galaxies are too far south to be seen from European latitudes. What are they called?

3 Who first proved that the objects formerly called spiral nebulæ are, in fact, external systems far beyond the Milky Way?

4 Give the 'odd one out': the Whirlpool, the Sombrero Hat, the Black-Eye, the Sword of Orion.

5 M.32 is also known as NGC 221. What does NGC mean?

6 The most remote object so far detected lies at a distance of (a) less than 10,000,000 light-years, (b) less than 5000 million light-years, (c) more than 10,000 million light-years.

7 Why are supernovæ useful in measuring the distances of galaxies?

8 What is a Seyfert galaxy, and why is it so named?

9 Which are the more remote: pulsars or quasars?
10 Explain the term 'Local Group'.

True or False?

1 All external galaxies are receding from the Sun and the Earth.
2 The universe is at least 10,000 million years old.
3 Only one quasar, 3C-273, is brighter than the 15th magnitude.
4 The elliptical galaxy M.87, in Virgo, is a strong radio source.
5 Our Milky Way galaxy is the largest galaxy known.
6 A BL Lacertæ object is a special kind of variable star.
7 The Tarantula Nebula is much larger than the Orion Nebula.
8 If it could be observed from the Andromeda Spiral, our Sun would appear about as bright as the planet Venus does to us.
9 Long-period variables (Mira stars) have been used to measure the distances of very remote galaxies.
10 The Whirlpool Galaxy lies in the constellation of Ursa Major, close to Alkaid (Eta Ursæ Majoris).

General knowledge: 1

1 What was the name of the European space-probe which went through the coma of Halley's Comet in March 1986?
2 Which of the nine planets has the longest revolution period?
3 Arrange the following bodies in order of size, beginning with the largest: Io, the Moon, Dione, Juno, Ganymede, Mercury, Leda.
4 Why does the Moon usually remain visible all through a total lunar eclipse?
5 What is the Saros?
6 Where is the Siding Spring Observatory?
7 What is the English name for the Gegenschein?
8 What do you understand by early and late type stars?
9 Name the south polar star.
10 Give the 'odd one out': Lilium, Antinoüs, Cerberus, Musca, Tarandus.

True or False?

1 There are ten external galaxies visible with the naked eye.
2 The nearest star beyond the Sun lies at a distance of one astronomical unit.
3 Most double stars are binary systems, not optical pairs (line of sight effects).
4 Swift's Comet is so named because of its rapid motion round the Sun.

5 The seasons are due to the changing position of the Moon in the sky.

6 The Sun's corona can be seen with the naked eye only during a total solar eclipse.

7 A circular crater on the Moon will appear elliptical if it lies near the lunar limb.

8 The maximum surface temperature on Mercury is lower than that on Venus.

9 Auroræ can never be seen from latitudes below 10° north or south.

10 The only month which can lack a new moon is February.

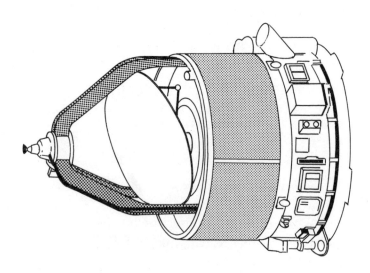

QUIZ
14

General knowledge: 2

1 The Northern Light is known as Aurora Borealis. What is the name for the Southern Light?

2 Name (a) the largest asteroid, (b) the brightest asteroid, (c) the asteroid which moves mainly between the orbits of Saturn and Uranus, (d) the asteroid which passed the Earth in 1937 at a distance less than twice that of the Moon, (e) the only two asteroids known to pass closer in to the Sun than the orbit of Mercury.

3 Explain the following terms: perihelion, perigee, quadrature, opposition, inferior conjunction, aphelion.

4 Which is the brightest crater on the Moon?

5 How long does light take to reach us from the Sun?

6 A new observatory has been set up on one of the Canary Islands. What is the name of the island?

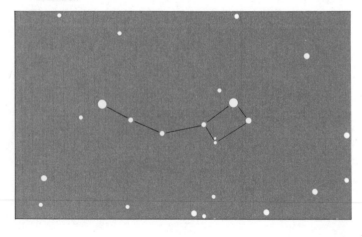

7 Who, or what, is the Via Lactea?
8 Give the spectral types of the following stars: Arcturus, Vega, Betelgeux, Antares, Pollux, Sirius.
9 What is the difference between an H.I region and an H.II region?
10 Why do stars twinkle more than planets?

True or False?

1 More than a thousand globular clusters are known in our Galaxy.
2 Richard West, discoverer of the bright comet of 1976, is a Danish astronomer.
3 There is only one constellation which has no star above the fifth magnitude.
4 The Pole Star takes 26,000 years to revolve round the Sun.
5 The first great Russian space pioneer was Konstantin Eduardovich Tchaikovsky.
6 The Earth is moving gradually closer to the Sun each year.
7 The Turkish flag shows the planet Venus together with the Moon.
8 Europa, the second large satellite of Jupiter, has a red surface and active volcanoes.
9 Wolf Creek Crater, in Australia, was formed by a plunging meteorite.
10 Phœbe was the Christian name of the American astronomer who discovered Pluto.

49

General knowledge: 3

1 What was the name of the Danish astronomer who was the first to measure the velocity of light?

2 On which planet would you look for the Great Red Spot?

3 Name the regions on Mars where *Viking 1* and *Viking 2* landed in 1976.

4 What is, or was, the Maunder Minimum?

5 Between August 1966 and August 1967 five space-probes were put into orbit round the Moon, and mapped almost the entire lunar surface. What was the name of this series of probes?

6 Who held the post of Astronomer Royal on 1 January 1987?

7 On which limb of the Moon is the Mare Orientale?

8 Give the 'odd one out': Gamma Crucis, Alphard, Aldebaran, Altair, Antares.

9 What important constellation is well seen from northern latitudes during autumn evenings, and has its four main stars arranged in a square?

10 In which American state is the McDonald Observatory?

True or False?

1 The Triangulum Spiral is larger than the Solar System.

2 Hyperion and Phœbe are the only satellites of Saturn to have retrograde motion.

3 The south celestial pole lies in the Large Cloud of Magellan.

4 Arcturus is the most luminous star known.

5 John Glenn was the first American to go into space.

6 John Flamsteed was the first Director of the Royal Greenwich Observatory.

7 There can sometimes be nine eclipses of the Sun in one calendar year.

8 Toro, only a few kilometres in diameter, moves round the Earth, and must therefore be regarded as a second Earth satellite.

9 The KAO is really a modified Lockheed C-141 aircraft carrying a 36-inch (91-centimetre) reflector. It can fly above 85 per cent of the Earth's atmosphere.

10 Between 1832 and 1838 Sir John Herschel, son of Sir William, took a large telescope to New South Wales to carry out a systematic study of the stars which are too far south to be seen from Britain.

General knowledge: 4

1 What happened to Biela's periodical comet, and where is it now?

2 How many known satellites has Neptune, and what are their names?

3 Where are Loki, Pele and Volund?

4 What are the objects once referred to as Red Flames?

5 For what do we best remember Bernhard Schmidt?

6 How many parsecs are there in a megaparsec?

7 What is the Blaze Star, and where is it?

8 In what constellations are the four stars making up the False Cross?

9 What are the proper names of the following stars: (a) Alpha Ceti, (b) Gamma Orionis, (c) Zeta Ursæ Majoris, (d) Alpha Eridani, (e) Alpha Virginis?

10 The Pulkovo Observatory is in (a) Czechoslovakia, (b) California, (c) the USSR, (d) Peru, (e) France.

True or False?

1 The furthest galaxies are often called pulsars.

2 If you could go to Alpha Centauri, the Sun would appear as a fairly bright star in the constellation of Cassiopeia.

3 Mira Ceti was the first famous American woman astronomer.

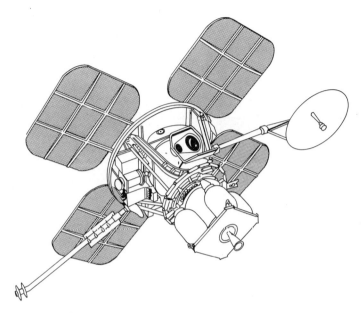

4 Only one space-probe, *Mariner 10*, has so far bypassed the planet Mercury.

5 *NASA* stands for the National Astronomy and Space Association.

6 *Apollo 13* landed on the Moon, near the crater Fra Mauro, in 1970.

7 The element helium was detected in the spectrum of the Sun before it was identified on the Earth.

8 Neptune is slightly larger and more massive than Uranus.

9 Phosphorus and Hesperus were old names for the planet Venus.

10 The first successful planetary probe was *Mariner 2*, which bypassed Venus in 1962.

QUIZ
17

General knowledge: 5

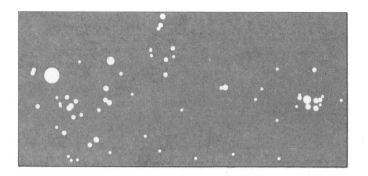

1 In which Leicestershire village did a meteorite
  fall on Christmas Eve 1965?
2 How many satellites in the Solar System are
  larger than the planet Mercury, if any?
3 What is the Black Drop, and when is it seen?
4 What are the English names for (a) Mare
  Nubium, (b) Sinus Æstuum, (c) Palus
  Nebularum, (d) Sinus Medii, (e) Mare
  Humboldtianum?
5 Who founded the Lowell Observatory in
  Flagstaff, Arizona?
6 Areography is (a) the study of stony
  meteorites, (b) a method of dating rocks by
  their radioactive content, (c) the geography of
  Mars, (d) a star-catalogue compiled by the
  Arabian astronomer Al-Sûfi in the year 950,
  (e) Mesopotamian astrology.
7 Classify the following variable stars: Chi Cygni,
  Beta Doradûs, R Hydræ, Beta Pegasi, Lambda
  Tauri.

8 What was the original name of the constellation Vulpecula?

9 If a star has positive radial motion, is it approaching or receding from the Earth?

10 Arrange the following objects in order of maximum apparent brightness: Venus, Mars, Jupiter, Capella, Sirius.

True or False?

1 Globular clusters contain fewer stars than open clusters.

2 The Owl Nebula and the Dumb-bell Nebula are galaxies in the Local Group.

3 The First Point of Aries lies in the constellation of the Ram.

4 Spica (in Virgo) looks brighter than Deneb (in Cygnus).

5 The barycentre lies 1707 kilometres below the surface of the Earth.

6 The world's largest single-mirror telescope is in the USSR.

7 Barrow and Birmingham are to be found on the Moon.

8 A total eclipse of the Sun was seen in England shortly before the Battle of Hastings in 1066.

9 The dark regions of Mars are old sea-beds, filled with low-type vegetation.

10 The first liquid-propellant rocket was fired by Robert Goddard in 1926.

Pot-pourri

1 Snickers is (a) a closely knitted garment worn by astronomers to protect themselves from the cold when observing at high altitude, (b) a dwarf galaxy, (c) an optical defect in Schmidt corrector plates, (d) a Jugoslav astrophysicist.
2 What will be the first day of the twenty-first century?
3 In what year did Galileo drop stones off the top of the Leaning Tower of Pisa, to demonstrate that all objects fall at an equal rate regardless of their weight?

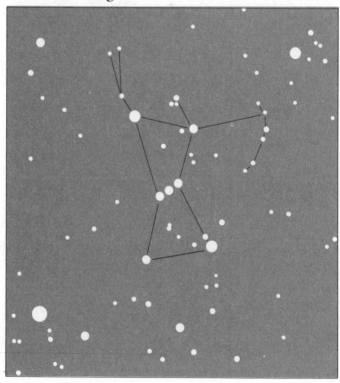

4 Where would you find the planet Vulcan in 1988?

5 An ocular is (a) a catlike animal commonly seen round the observatory at Mauna Kea in Hawaii, (b) a type of galaxy which emits very little radiation in the optical range, (c) an old form of transit instrument, (d) a telescopic eyepiece, (d) a seventeenth-century work on optics.

6 How many annular eclipses of the Moon can be seen in one calendar year? (Give the maximum number.)

7 Who was Jep?

8 Polyhymnia is (a) a Greek mathematician, (b) a disease of the eye caused by excessive telescopic usage, (c) the city in which Ptolemy was living when he wrote the *Almagest*, (d) an asteroid.

9 What insects were deliberately removed by a stonemason from the columns at the entrance to the Yerkes Observatory before the official opening of the Observatory – and why?

10 What famous comedian discovered a white spot on Saturn in 1933?

True or False?

1 An achondrite is an astronomer who refuses to accept the existence of God.

2 The Red Shift is the Soviet plan for moving their main telescopes to the Caucasus region of the USSR, where observing conditions are comparatively favourable.

3 The star Arcturus sends us about as much heat as a single candle would do from a distance of 5 miles (8 kilometres).

4 The Gum Nebula in the constellation of Vela is so named because it contains molecules which, under terrestrial conditions, would be sticky.

5 Forbidden lines are works condemned as heretical by the Inquisition before the trial of Galileo in 1634.

6 An Astronomer Royal once publicly burned all the copies of a particular astronomical work which fell into his hands.

7 Ra-Shalom was an Egyptian astronomer who was one of the first to maintain that the Earth revolves round the Sun.

8 The aerial used by Karl Jansky to detect radio waves from the Milky Way was made partly from the parts of a dismantled Morris car.

9 A junior member of the Astronomical Society of South Africa is often referred to as a white dwarf.

10 The world's most advanced transit instrument is named after a type of beer.

For the expert

1 A thalassoid is (a) a light-floored walled plain on the far side of the Moon, (b) a mathematical inequality in the Moon's motion, (c) an armadillo-like creature found in the region of Cape Canaveral, (d) an Arabian astrologer, (e) the secondary mirror of a Cassegrain reflector.

2 Why is the largest crater on Mars' satellite Phobos named Stickney?

3 Name the two largest basins in the southern hemisphere of Mars.

4 The constellation of Delphinus is named in honour of the dolphin who, in legend, rescued a famous singer from drowning. What was the name of the singer?

5 Give the 'odd one out': R Carinæ, R Leporis, R Aræ, R Cassiopeiæ, R Trianguli.
6 In 1962, for the first time, two cosmonauts in separate spacecraft were in orbit round the Earth simultaneously. Who were they?
7 What is Spörer's Law?
8 In the constellation Aquila, how many stars are there above magnitude 3.5? (a) None, (b) 4, (c) 6, (d) 2, (e) 7.
9 Give the proper names of the following stars: Beta Carinæ, Theta Eridani, Eta Virginis, Sigma Sagittarii, Alpha Crateris.
10 What is Hubble's Constant, and what is its approximate value?

True or False?

1 Celestial latitude is another name for declination.
2 The Gottorp Globe is an ancient orrery, discovered at Göteborg in Sweden in 1895.
3 An inferior planet is an asteroid less than 10 kilometres in diameter.
4 Two nineteenth-century astronomers were also well known as engineers; James Nasmyth invented the steam-hammer, and W. C. Bond invented the flush lavatory.

5 When the Ulster Railway was being built in the mid-nineteenth century, the originally planned track was diverted to avoid Armagh Observatory, because the observatory director complained that passing trains would shake his telescopes.

6 Julian days are named in honour of Julius Cæsar, who was responsible for an important reform of the calendar.

7 The revolution period of the binary Gamma Virginis is approximately 171 years.

8 Goethe, Beethoven, Chopin and Ibsen are to be found on the planet Mercury.

9 The constellation Circinus adjoins Centaurus, Ara and Triangulum Australe.

10 Bode's Law was discovered by Johann Elert Bode in 1772.

QUIZ

20

Try this, then!

1 Where are: (a) Modred, (b) Izanagi,
(c) Roncevaux Terra, (d) Thrace Macula,
(e) Asgard?

2 Who was the only Director of the Natal
Observatory?

 3 In which constellations are (a) M.87 (b) M.81
(c) M.67 (d) M.32 (e) M.102?

4 Which observatory building was paid for by
the sale of old and decayed gunpowder?

5 Give the 'odd one out': Aristillus, Alphonsus,
Autolycus, Timocharis, Lambert.

6 Who named the stars Alpha and Beta Delphini,
and what are the proper names?

7 What is the official name of the periodical
comet formerly known as Pons-Coggia-
Winnecke-Forbes?

8 Name (a) Asteroid No. 433, (b) the astronomer
whose brother, Meyerbeer, was a famous
composer, (c) the rocket research establishment
once bombed by the RAF, (d) the largest crater
on Saturn's satellite Mimas, (e) the third
Astronomer Royal.

9 What is notable about a tektite found in 1932
at Muong Nong, Laos?

10 What is the proper name of the star 80 Ursæ
Majoris?

True or False?

1 A director of the Paris Observatory was dismissed in 1870 because of his rudeness.

2 Phobos and Deimos have revolution periods of less than one sol.

3 The Moon has three liberations: (a) liberation in longitude, (b) liberation in latitude, (c) diurnal liberation.

4 The heliopause is the period of solar minimum, when spot-groups are rare. It lasts for about three years.

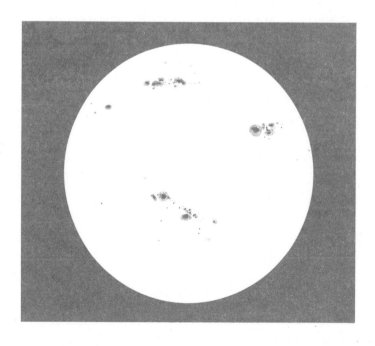

5 In 1987 the Einstein Observatory was visited by 4000 people.
6 The Celestial Police were the guards sent by the Pope to arrest Galileo, in 1633, and bring him to Rome for trial on a charge of heresy.
7 The La Silla Observatory, in Chile, is named after a Marxist revolutionary leader.
8 The constellation Ursa Major covers more square degrees of the sky than Virgo.
9 In August 1976 the Russian probe *Luna 24* went to the Moon, landed in the Mare Crisium, and then returned to Earth, bringing samples of lunar material.
10 Members of the Hirayama family are Japanese bankers who have financed the observatories at Tokyo, Kyoto and Osaka.

THE ANSWERS

QUIZ 1

1 A star is a self-luminous body; a normal star is a globe of hot gas radiating at a furious rate. A planet has no light of its own, and is a relatively small body moving round a star. It is fair to say that the Sun is a typical star, while the Earth is a typical planet.

2 In round figures, 24 hours; the actual period is 23 hours, 56 minutes, 4 seconds. This is the rotation period relative to the stars, so that if a star is due south at a certain time to an observer on the Earth's surface it will again be due south 23 hours, 56 minutes, 4 seconds later. Since a civil day is equal to 24 hours, it follows that a star will rise about 4 minutes earlier each day. Note that astronomically a 'day' is the full rotational period, not merely the time when the Sun is above the observer's horizon.

3 In round figures, 365 days; actually 365 days, 6 hours, 9 minutes, 10 seconds.

4 Orbit means 'path'. Thus the Earth is in orbit round the Sun.

5 No. Some star-groups are visible from both hemispheres; but from England we can never see the far-southern groups such as the Southern Cross, while from Australia you can never see the far-northern groups such as the Little Bear.

6 Yes. Unmanned vehicles have landed on Venus and Mars, and have bypassed Venus, Mars, Mercury, Jupiter, Saturn and Uranus.

7 Yes, very often. The waning crescent Moon will remain in the morning sky well after sunrise, and the waxing crescent Moon will rise well before sunset.

8 Yes; at 186,000 miles (300,000 kilometres) per second.

9 Because the Earth spins on its axis from west to east.

10 Sirius, which is a star; all the others are planets.

True or False?

1 False! Greenwich Observatory is Britain's leading *astronomical* institution. Astronomy is the science of the sky; astrology, the superstition of the sky, has no basis whatsoever, and is a pseudo-science strictly for the credulous only.

2 True, though it is not very efficient; it reflects on average only seven per cent of the sunlight falling on to its surface.

3 True. The Sun is a typical star.

4 False. Gravity becomes weaker with increased distance from the Earth, but in theory the Earth's gravitational field is infinite. Remember that the Moon stays together with us because of the effect of the Earth's gravitational pull.

5 False. The Sun is the central body of the Solar System, but not of the universe.

6 False. A comet lies far beyond the Earth's atmosphere, at a distance of millions of miles or kilometres, and you have to watch it for a considerable period before you can detect any motion against the starry background.

7 False. The Moon is much more distant than any cloud!

8 True. The blue part of the Sun's light is more easily scattered than the red part; if you fly in a high-altitude jet aircraft you will see that the sky is becoming darker, because there is less atmosphere above you. From an airless world the sky would be black even in the daytime.

9 True, by about 3,000,000 miles (almost 5,000,000 kilometres), but the seasons are due to the tilt of the Earth's axis of rotation, not to our changing distance from the Sun.

10 True. The planets travel slowly round the sky, moving from one constellation to another, although they always keep within well defined limits.

QUIZ 2

1 A satellite is really a 'secondary body' moving round a planet. Our Earth has only one natural satellite, the Moon.

2 The Sun, which is the central body of the Solar System. (We may ourselves regard the Earth as the most important inasmuch as we live here, but on the cosmic scale the Earth is a very insignificant body indeed.)

3 A constellation is a group of stars in the sky. Thousands of years ago, the ancient astronomers divided up the stars into patterns, and each pattern was named, often after a living creature or a mythological character, but these names are quite arbitrary, and different civilizations had different constellations – though the stars, of course, were the

same. Moreover, the stars are not equally distant from us, so that a constellation has no real significance, and the stars in any particular constellation merely happen to lie in more or less the same direction as seen from the Earth.

4 Polaris, the north polar star, which lies within one degree of the north celestial pole. It can never be seen from New Zealand, because it always remains below the horizon there.

5 Escape velocity is the initial velocity which would have to be given to a body escaping from the gravitational pull of a larger body. For the Earth it is 7 miles per second (11 kilometres per second). Thus if a rocket (or any other object) is sent upward from the Earth at a speed of 7 miles (11 kilometres) per second, it will never return; if it is given a lower initial velocity it will not be able to break free from the Earth's gravitational pull.

6 The stars are much further away than the planets. Even the nearest star beyond the Sun lies at a distance of over four light-years.

7 No. Above an altitude of 120 miles (200 kilometres) or so the density of the Earth's air is negligible – and it is over 230,000 miles (370,000 kilometres) to the Moon.

8 The Galaxy is the star-system of which our Sun is a member. It contains around 100,000 million stars.

9 (b) is correct.

10 Yes. The way to find out whether any particular year is a leap year is to divide by 4; if there is no remainder, we have a leap year. The only exception to

this rule is that a 'century year' must be divisible by 400. Thus 1900 was not a leap year, but 2000 will be.

True or False?

1 False. It has been suggested that the Moon may have some effect upon the weather, but the evidence is very uncertain, and even if an effect does exist it is very slight indeed.

2 False. All these three are comparatively small planets.

3 True. For six months in the year the Sun is south of the celestial equator, and does not set over the south pole; for the other six months it is north of the equator, and remains below the horizon from the south pole.

4 False. The stars are suns in their own right.

5 True. To look straight at the Sun through any telescope or binoculars is extremely dangerous, even if a dark filter is used. All the Sun's light (and, more importantly, heat) is focused on to the observer's eye, and the results are bound to be disastrous. No dark filter can give proper protection, and is also liable to shatter at any moment. There is only one golden rule for looking straight at the Sun through any optical equipment (even a camera lens); *don't*.

6 True; much closer. Artificial satellites move round the Earth at distances of a few hundreds of miles (or kilometres) or at most a few thousands.

7 False. One cannot see stars in the daytime because there is insufficient contrast between the star's

brightness and the sky brightness; looking from the bottom of a well makes absolutely no difference.

8 False. Men have been to the Moon, but not (yet) to Mars.

9 False. A shooting-star, or meteor, is a small particle burning out in the Earth's upper atmosphere. It has no relationship with a real star.

10 True. Iceland, on the borders of the Arctic Circle, has a much longer daylight period during northern summer than Spain. (The Arctic Circle grazes the northern part of Iceland, and passes through the island of Grimsay.)

QUIZ 3

1 Claudius Ptolemæus, better remembered as Ptolemy. He died around the year AD 180. According to the Ptolemaic system, the Sun, Moon, planets and stars all revolved round the Earth.

2 Nicolaus Copernicus – or in Polish, Mikołaj Kopernik.

3 Isaac Newton; the great book was published in 1687.

4 Yuri Gagarin, in April 1961. He made one complete circuit of the Earth in *Vostok 1*.

5 Ryle, who was English; all the others were American.

6 Galileo Galilei. Note that I said the first 'great' astronomer. Galileo was not the first observer to use a

telescope astronomically, but he was undoubtedly the greatest.

7 James Gregory, in 1663. Gregory, a Scottish mathematician, never actually made a reflector (as he admitted, he had no practical skill) and the first reflector was made by Newton, who presented it to the Royal Society in 1671.

8 Friedrich Wilhelm Bessel, of Königsberg Observatory.

9 Tycho Brahe, Sir Arthur (Stanley) Eddington, Sir Harold Spencer Jones, Sir Fred Hoyle, Camille Flammarion. (Note that 'Fred' is not short for Frederick or Alfred; Hoyle was christened Fred.)

10 Wernher von Braun.

True or False?

1 True. There may have been earlier telescopes (probably there were), but Lippershey's was the first about whose existence we can be absolutely certain.

2 True. He was Professor of Astronomy at Oxford long before he turned over to architecture.

3. False. There has been no woman Astronomer Royal. Dr Margaret Burbidge acted as Director of the Royal Greenwich Observatory for a brief period in succession to Sir Richard Woolley, but without the title of Astronomer Royal.

4 True: Tycho Brahe, who set up his observatory at Hven, in the Baltic, in 1576 and remained there until 1596. The prison was installed to incarcerate tenants who refused to pay their rents. In his youth Tycho had

part of his nose sliced off in a duel, and fashioned himself a false one.

5 False. Relativity theory was developed by Albert Einstein. Jacob Epstein was a sculptor.

6 False. Kepler's first two Laws were published in 1609, not 1709 (the third was published in 1618).

7 False; Conrad was the third. He was commander of *Apollo 12* (November 1969). He had been preceded by Armstrong and Aldrin in *Apollo 11* (July 1969).

8 False. Different constellation patterns had been drawn up much earlier by the Chinese, Egyptians, Mesopotamians and Greeks. It is however true that we use today the Latin names of the Greek constellations.

9 True. The heliacal rising of Sirius gave the Egyptians the key to the annual flooding of the Nile, which was vital to their economy.

10 False – but only just! Minor Planet No. 518 was discovered by R. S. Dugan, who named it Halawe after an Arabian sweet of which he was particularly fond.

QUIZ 4

1 A type of telescope mounting designed to avoid the need for moving in both altitude (up or down) and azimuth (east to west). There are various forms, but essentially there is a polar axis, directed to the celestial pole, and a declination axis, supporting the telescope at right angles to the polar axis. When the telescope is turned on the polar axis, the altitude correction looks after itself, so that only one motion is needed. If a

QUIZ FOUR

driving mechanism is added to move the telescope at a rate sufficient to compensate for the Earth's rotation, the target object will remain in the field of view.

2 The INT is the Isaac Newton Telescope. It was originally set up at the Royal Greenwich Observatory, Herstmonceux, with a 96-inch (244-centimetre) mirror. It has since been moved to the new observatory in the Canary Islands, and given a slightly larger mirror with an aperture of 100.8 inches (256 centimetres).

3 At the Yerkes Observatory in the United States. It has an object-glass 40 inches (101.6 centimetres) in diameter.

4 In Cheshire, England.

5 The 72-inch (182.7-centimetre) reflector made by the third Earl of Rosse in 1845. It was then much the most powerful in the world.

6 UKIRT (the United Kingdom Infra-Red Telescope) is on Mauna Kea, in Hawaii.

7 It carried an X-ray telescope, UHURU was the first really successful X-ray satellite, and detected 160 discrete sources – many of them in our Galaxy, but also some in external systems.

8 In the seventeenth century: to be precise, in 1675, by order of King Charles II. At that time, sailors out of sight of land frequently lost their bearings because they could not find their longitude. Latitude could be found easily enough, but longitude was much more troublesome. The only way to do it seemed to be by making observations of the changing position of the Moon against the stars. Obviously a good star-catalogue was needed, and the best one then available

(Tycho Brahe's) was still not good enough. Therefore, the King gave orders for a new observatory to be established so that a better star-catalogue could be compiled. This was duly done, though by the time the catalogue was finished the problem of longitude-finding had been solved in another way. Subsequently the Observatory became a major astronomical establishment, though it has remained the 'timekeeping centre of the world'.

9 Because it is to be put into an orbit round the Earth, above the top of the main atmosphere, and will have perfect seeing conditions. It will have a 94-inch (239-centimetre) mirror, and will be a 'free flyer', operated by remote control.

10 All are in Chile, where observing conditions are exceptionally good.

True or False?

1 False. An instrument for splitting up light is a spectroscope. An interferometer depends upon the principle of light interference.

2 False. A transit instrument moves only in altitude, and always points due north/south. The moment at which a star passes over the observer's meridian can be determined very accurately, and this in turn gives the precise time at that moment.

3 False. The Palomar telescope is known as the Hale reflector.

4 False. Mirrors cannot be made from untreated portholes – though it is true that portholes have been

81

used as blanks for the mirrors of comparatively small reflectors.

5 True. The telescope has a mirror 236 inches (600 centimetres) in diameter. It must be admitted that it has not proved to be very satisfactory, though efforts to improve its performance are now being made.

6 True. The Denver High Altitude Observatory at Boulder is at an altitude of 14,097 feet (4296 metres). It is thus slightly higher than the observatory on the summit of Mauna Kea.

7 True. The planetarium was completed in 1923.

8 False. The Helwan Observatory is in Egypt (lat. 29°51′31″N, long. 31°21′E).

9 True. One can only hope that the closure will not be permanent.

10 False. It means that each main lens is 7 millimetres in diameter, and that the magnifying power is 50.

QUIZ 5

1 93 million miles or 150 million kilometres. (To be precise, the mean Earth–Sun distance is 92,957,000 miles or 149,593,000 kilometres.)

2 Because it is some 3600°F (2000°C) cooler than the surrounding bright surface. If a sunspot could be seen shining on its own, its surface brightness would be greater than that of an arc-lamp.

3 Fraunhofer lines are dark lines in the spectrum of the Sun. They are named in honour of the German

optician Josef Fraunhofer, who first studied them in detail in the years following 1814.

The light from the Sun can be split up by means of a spectroscope. The bright surface produces a rainbow band (if a slit is used) from red at the long-wave end through to violet at the short-wave end. Above the bright surface are cooler gases, and these gases produce the dark lines. Each line is due to some definite substance, and each substance has therefore its own 'trade-mark' which cannot be duplicated, so that we can tell which elements are present in the Sun. For example, two prominent dark lines in the yellow part of the spectrum can be due only to sodium.

4 No; the Sun is not burning in the accepted sense of the term. It is producing its energy by nuclear reactions taking place deep inside it.

The Sun contains a great deal of hydrogen, which is the lightest of all the elements and is also the most plentiful substance in the whole universe. Near the Sun's core, where the temperatures and pressures are tremendous, the hydrogen is being changed into the next lightest element, helium. It takes four hydrogen atoms to make one atom of helium; each time this happens, a little energy is released – and it is this energy which keeps the Sun shining. (Strictly speaking, we should say that it takes four hydrogen *nuclei* to make one helium nucleus, because inside the Sun the atoms are ionized – that is to say, the electrons which move round the nucleus are stripped off.)

5 About 225,000,000 years – a period sometimes called the 'cosmic year'. One cosmic year ago, the most advanced life-forms on Earth were amphibians. Even the dinosaurs had yet to make their entry.

6 (a) Total, when the bright surface of the Sun is fully covered by the Moon. (b) Partial, when only part of the Sun is covered. (c) Annular (from the Latin *annulus*, a ring), when the alignment is perfect but the Moon is near its greatest distance from the Earth; it then appears slightly smaller than the Sun, so that a ring of sunlight is left showing round the dark disk of the Moon. Of course, there is a partial zone on Earth to either side of the central track of a total eclipse, and some eclipses may be total along part of their track and annular along the rest of the track.

7 The photosphere is the visible bright surface of the Sun, on which sunspots appear.

8 At the (northern) summer solstice, around 21 June each year.

9 Type G2. (I think we may accept simply 'G'!)

10 A periodical cycle of the Sun's behaviour. At maximum the Sun is very active, with many spot-groups and associated phenomena. Activity then declines to minimum before picking up once more; near minimum (as in 1987) the disk may be without spots for many consecutive days. The cycle is not perfectly regular, but the mean period is 11 years; it has ranged between 17.1 years (1788 to 1805) and 7.3 years (1829.9 to 1837).

In fact, there are grounds for believing that the true cycle is 22 years, or two maxima and two minima, so we may allow either answer.

True or False?

1 True. The Pole Star is at least 7000 times more luminous than the Sun – but it is about 680 light-years away.

2 False. The last total eclipse visible from England was on 29 June 1927. (The eclipse of 30 June 1954 just missed the British Isles; the track of totality ran north of Scotland into Scandinavia. Over England a large partial eclipse was seen.)

3 False. However, the Earth–Sun distance was once measured by observations of transits of Venus, and, latterly, by measuring the distance of Venus by using radar. Once the distance of Venus is known, that of the Sun can be calculated from Kepler's Laws.

4 True. The particles from the Sun cascade down into the Earth's upper air and cause the lovely glows. Because they are electrified, the particles are attracted to the magnetic poles, which is why auroræ are best seen from high latitudes – though it must be added that the whole process is rather more complicated than used to be thought.

5 False. The loss of mass is four *million* tons a second. (Please do not be alarmed. The Sun has enough mass to last it for a very long time yet!)

6 False. The surface temperature is rather below 10,800°F (6000°C). The temperature at the core has been given as over 27,000,000°F (15,000,000°C); recent evidence indicates that this may be slightly too high, but in any case it is well over 90,000°F (50,000°C).

85

7 False. The solar wind has nothing to do with meteorology, or with a conventional wind; it is made up of a stream of electrified particles being sent out by the Sun constantly in all directions.

8 True. The observatory is at Homestake Mine, near Deadwood Gulch in South Dakota.

The Sun is a source of neutrinos, which are particles with no electric charge and no mass (or at least, virtually none). They are thus very difficult to 'trap', but they may betray their presence by interacting with atoms of chlorine. At Homestake Mine, Dr Raymond Davies and his colleagues have a large tank filled with tetrachloroethylene (cleaning fluid) which is rich in chlorine; periodically the tank is examined to see how many chlorine atoms have been hit by neutrons. So far, it seems that there are fewer neutrinos than theory predicts. The experiment has to be carried out deep below ground level, as otherwise the results would be confused by cosmic ray particles – which, however, cannot penetrate a mile of solid rock.

9 False. A solar eclipse can happen only at new moon, when the Earth, Sun and Moon are lined up with the Moon in the mid position. At these times, of course, the night side of the Moon is turned toward us.

10 True. The Sun's volume is 1,303,600 times that of the Earth.

QUIZ 6

1 27 days (to be precise, 27.321 days). However, because both Earth and Moon are in orbit round the

Sun, the interval between successive new moons (or successive full moons) is 29 days, 12 hours, 44 minutes.

2 A lunar eclipse is caused when the Moon passes into the cone of shadow cast by the Earth, and its supply of direct sunlight is temporarily cut off.

3 Because the Moon has what is termed synchronous or captured rotation. As we have seen, it goes round the Earth in 27.3 days; this is also the time taken for the Moon to spin once on its axis, so that it has a very slow 'day'. The result is that it keeps the same face turned toward the Earth all the time. To show what is meant, walk round a chair, turning so as to keep your face turned toward the chair. Anyone sitting on the chair will never see the back of your neck – but you are nevertheless rotating, because during your circuit you will have faced every wall of the room. It is much the same with the Earth and the Moon, though because the Moon's orbit is not quite circular, and hence its velocity in orbit varies, there is a slight 'rocking' motion which enables us to see a little way around the mean edge of the Moon at different times. All in all, we can examine 59 per cent of the whole surface, though of course never more than 50 per cent at any one time. The remaining 41 per cent is permanently averted. There is no mystery about this synchronous behaviour; tidal friction over the ages has been responsible. In its early history the Moon must have been viscous instead of solid, and the Earth's pull of gravity raised tides in it. As the Moon spun, it had to fight against the Earth's pull, which tended to keep a tidal bulge turned Earthward. The Moon's spin was slowed down, until relative to the Earth it had stopped

altogether. Note, however, that the rotation has not stopped relative to the Sun, so that it is quite wrong to suppose that one side of the Moon is permanently dark.

4 The Moon is virtually without atmosphere. This is because the lunar escape velocity – 1.5 miles (2.4 kilometres) per second – is too low for the Moon to have held down any atmosphere it may once have had.

5 The Mare Tranquillitatis (Sea of Tranquillity).

6 An occultation occurs when the Moon passes in front of a star, or other celestial object. Occultations of stars are useful, because they give the Moon's position in the sky at the moment of occultation – bearing in mind that until recently, at any rate, the apparent positions of the stars were better known than the motions of the Moon. Strictly speaking, an eclipse of the Sun is an occultation of the Sun by the Moon.

7 Pico, which is a mountain. All the others are craters.

8 Sinus Iridum: Bay of Rainbows. Mare Nubium: Sea of Clouds. Lacus Mortis: Lake of Death. Mare Frigoris: Sea of Cold. Oceanus Procellarum: Ocean of Storms.

9 The regolith is the loose upper layer of the Moon's surface, approximately 3–65 feet (1–20 metres) deep; on average 13–50 feet (4–15 metres) in the maria, 30 feet (9 metres) in the highlands. It is a breccia, containing many different ingredients. Below it is a layer of shattered bedrock.

10 Commander Eugene Cernan, from *Apollo 17*, in December 1972.

True or False?

1 False. There are five larger satellites: Io, Ganymede and Callisto in Jupiter's system, Titan in Saturn's, and Triton in Neptune's. (The diameter of Triton is not accurately known, but is almost certainly greater than that of the Moon.)

2 False. Hell is a normal lunar crater, 20 miles (32 kilometres) in diameter, with a low central peak; it is not particularly deep. It is named after a last-century Hungarian astronomer, Maximilian Hell, and has nothing to do with the Inferno!

3 True. The pictures, sent back in October 1959, gave the first views of the Moon's far side.

4 False. The Moon has no detectable overall magnetic field, though there may have been one in the remote past, and there are localized areas of magnetized material.

5 False. The so-called Soviet Mountains, recorded by *Luna 3* in 1959, do not exist; what was thought to be a mountain range proved to be a bright ray.

6 False. It is true that most people believe the low-down full moon to be larger than the higher-up full moon; but this is a well-known illusion, as any careful measurement will show. The illusion has been known for thousands of years!

7 True. Since the Moon has no atmosphere, there is nothing to scatter the blue part of the Sun's light.

8 False. Julius Cæsar, Vasco da Gama, Neil Armstrong and H. G. Wells have craters named after them, but Sir Winston Churchill has not.

9 False. The barycentre is the centre of gravity of the Earth–Moon system. Since it lies well within the Earth's globe, the simple statement that 'the Moon revolves round the Earth' is good enough for most purposes.

10 False. No major lunar craters have been formed in recorded times (suggestions to the contrary must be taken with a very large grain of cosmic salt!) and the Moon has been inactive for at least a thousand million years, though no doubt small impact craters have been formed occasionally.

QUIZ 7

1 Mercury, Venus, the Earth, Mars, Jupiter, Saturn, Uranus, Pluto, Neptune. (I agree that this is a catch. Pluto is normally the outermost planet, but its eccentric orbit brings it closer in than Neptune when it is near perihelion. Perihelion is due in 1989, and not until 1999 will Pluto regain its title of 'the outermost planet'.)

2 Venus, which can approach us within 25 million miles (40 million kilometres). Mars can never come much closer than 35 million miles (56 million kilometres).

3 The Earth! The canals reported on Mars by observers such as Percival Lowell were nothing more than optical illusions.

4 Mercury and Venus, which are closer to the Sun than we are.

5 Mars. Olympus Mons is a lofty volcano; Syrtis Major, the most conspicuous of the dark areas, is a plateau; and Valles Marineris is a tremendous valley.

6 Io, Europa, Ganymede and Callisto.

7 Iris, which is an asteroid. All the rest are planetary satellites.

8 Jupiter: 10 hours. To be more precise, the mean rotation of the equatorial zone is 9 hours, $50\frac{1}{2}$ minutes, and of the rest of the planet 9 hours, $55\frac{3}{4}$ minutes. Jupiter does not spin as a solid body would do, and in addition various definite features, such as spots, have rotation periods of their own, so that they drift around in longitude.

9 (a) Jupiter, with an equatorial diameter of over 88,000 miles (141,000 kilometres). (b) Pluto, whose diameter is now thought to be only about 1370 miles (2200 kilometres), appreciably smaller than Mercury and also smaller than several planetary satellites. (c) Uranus. (d) Jupiter; the main dipole field has a strength of about 4 gauss, as against 0.3 to 0.8 gauss at the surface of the Earth. (e) Uranus.

10 Ceres, Pallas, Juno and Vesta.

True or False?

1 False, though until the 1960s it was believed to be true. The revolution period of Mercury is 88 days, and if the rotation period were also 88 days there would be a region of permanent sunlight and a region of permanent night, with a narrow intervening 'twilight zone'. In fact the rotation period is only 58.6 days –

two-thirds of a Mercurian 'year' – so that every part of the planet is in sunlight at one time or another.

2 True. It was discovered by G. D. Cassini in 1675.

3 False. The markings were first seen telescopically in 1659 by Christiaan Huygens. Vastitas Borealis is the north polar plain of Mars, extending all round the planet and from latitude 55°N to 70°N.

4 False. The main asteroid belt lies between the orbits of Mars and Jupiter.

5 False. Uranus (magnitude 5.7) is just visible with the naked eye. Neptune (magnitude 7.7) is below naked-eye visibility, though binoculars will show it.

6 True. Asteroid 1604 is named Tombaugh; Asteroid 2602 is named Moore.

7 False. *Voyager 1* will never return, because it is moving too fast; it will leave the Solar System forever, and eventually we will lose track of it, though radio contact should be maintained well into the 1990s.

8 True. The last transit of Venus was that of 1882. Assuming that one's memory can go back to the age of three, this means that anyone who can remember the transit must have been born in 1879 or earlier.

9 False. The ground pressure of the Martian atmosphere is below 10 millibars everywhere – very much less than that at the summit of Everest.

10 True. *Pioneer 10*, launched in March 1972, made its closest pass of Jupiter on 3 December 1973, at a distance from the planet of 82,000 miles (132,000 kilometres).

1 (b) is correct. Therefore when a comet is moving outward from the Sun, it travels tail-first.

2 1910 and 1835.

3 No. Many faint comets do not develop tails, and there are even some comets which look almost stellar in appearance.

4 (a) The French astronomer Hervé Faye, in 1843. The period is 7.4 years, and the comet has been seen regularly since its discovery. (b) Pierre Méchain, the French comet-hunter, in 1786; it was recovered in 1795 by Caroline Herschel, in 1805 by Thulis and in 1818 by Pons before its periodicity was recognized. (c) Heinrich Ludwig D'Arrest, in 1851. The comet's period is 6.2 years, and it has been seen regularly. At its brightest it may just become visible with the naked eye.

5 The point in the sky from which the meteors of any particular shower seem to diverge. The reason is that the meteors of the shower are really travelling through space in parallel paths. The best everyday comparison is to stand on a bridge overlooking a motorway, and note how the parallel lanes of the motorway seem to issue from a point near the observer's horizon. Cars coming down the lanes will seem to diverge from that point – just as the shower meteors seem to diverge from their radiant.

6 (a) January (1 to 6). (b) August (25 July to 18 August). (c) November (15 to 19).

7 Donati's Comet.

8 In Arizona; lat. 35°3′N, long. 111°2′W. It is a well-known tourist attraction, within easy access of Highway 99.

9 A meteor which is not associated with any known shower. Sporadic meteors may appear from any direction at any moment.

10 A vast collection of comets orbiting the Sun at a distance of at least a light-year. According to J. H. Oort, who first proposed its existence, a comet in this cloud may be perturbed by some agency – a passing star, for example, or even a remote planet – and will then start to swing inward toward the Sun. After a journey lasting for thousands or even millions of years it will pass through perihelion, and if it is not 'captured' or violently perturbed by a planet, usually Jupiter, it will return to the cloud. If it is 'captured' it may be forced into a short-period orbit; there are also comets which have been perturbed by a planet and expelled from the Solar System. There is no definite proof of the existence of the Oort Cloud, but it does seem to fit the facts, and most authorities believe in it.

True or False?

1 False. The average meteor is no larger than a grain of sand.

2 False. There is absolutely no connection between thunderstorms, which are purely meteorological phenomena, and meteorites, which come from beyond the Earth's atmosphere. It is unfortunate, perhaps, that the name 'meteorology' for weather science suggests an association with meteors or meteorites.

3 False. Kohoutek's Comet, discovered on 7 March 1973 by Dr Lubos Kohoutek from Hamburg Observatory, was expected to become brilliant, but failed to do so; it was not easy to see with the naked eye. It may do better at its next return, which is due around the year AD 75,000!

4 True. Indeed, some cometary heads are larger than the Sun. The coma of the Great Comet of 1811 seems to have been 1,200,000 miles (2,000,000 kilometres) in diameter.

5 False. Halley's Comet returned at least seven years before the accepted date of Christ's birth; it was well documented by contemporary astronomers, and anyone could have seen it.

6 True; it is at Hoba West, near Grootfontein.

7 False. They were very rich in 1866 and 1966, but not in 1899 or 1933, because the Earth missed the main part of the meteor swarm. However, there is every prospect of another brilliant Leonid display on 17 November 1999. Generally the Leonids are spectacular every $33\frac{1}{3}$ years, and records of them go back to the year 902. A few Leonids are seen every year around 17 November.

8 False. An aerolite is a stony meteorite, probably coming from the asteroid belt.

9 True. Encke's Comet has the shortest period and the smallest orbit of any known periodical comet, and modern instruments can follow it even at aphelion.

10 False. There is no reliable evidence that any human being has been killed or seriously injured by a

meteorite, though it is true that one or two people have had narrow escapes, and an Egyptian dog was unlucky enough to be in the wrong place at the wrong time.

QUIZ 9

1 Ursa Major (in English, the Great Bear).

2 Capella.

3 You wouldn't – and indeed, during northern summer evenings Orion cannot be seen from anywhere, because the Sun is too close to it in the sky, and it is above the horizon only during broad daylight.

4 Cygnus (the Swan), which is the only one of these constellations not in the Zodiac.

5 Canopus (magnitude -0.72); Alpha Centauri (-0.27); Rigel (0.12); Deneb (1.25); Polaris (1.99).

6 Microscopium: the Microscope. Canes Venatici: the Hunting Dogs. Monoceros: the Unicorn. Aquila: the Eagle. Lacerta: the Lizard.

7 (a) Aldebaran (Alpha Tauri). (b) Sirius (Alpha Canis Majoris). (c) Mira (Omicron Ceti). (d) Mu Cephei. (e) Alphard (Alpha Hydræ).

8 Thuban (Alpha Draconis). It is no longer the pole star because the north celestial pole has since been shifted, by the effect known as precession. As the Earth spins, it is 'wobbling' very slowly in the manner of a gyroscope which is starting to topple. The effect is very

slight, but over the centuries it becomes appreciable. Today, the Earth's axis points northward to a point within one degree of Polaris. In 12,000 years' time Vega will be the north pole star.

9 (a) Regulus. (b) Alcyone. (c) Mizar. (d) Antares. (e) Castor.

10 (a) No. (b) No. (c) Yes, just. (d) Yes. (e) Yes.
In theory, Canopus can be seen from anywhere south of latitude 37°N, so that it does not rise from Athens (38°N) but does from Cairo (30°N). From Auckland it just about touches the horizon when at its lowest; from Invercargill, in the south of New Zealand (latitude 46°S), Canopus never sets.

True or False?

1 False. Saturn travels all the way round the Zodiac.

2 True; it covers only 68 square degrees. The next smallest constellation is Equuleus (72 square degrees).

3 False. In 1603 Johann Bayer allotted Greek letters to the stars in the constellations, theoretically beginning with the brightest (Alpha, Beta, Gamma . . .) and so on to Omega, the last letter of the Greek alphabet. In many cases the brightest star is indeed Alpha – thus Sirius is Alpha Canis Majoris, or Alpha of the Great Dog – but in many other cases the rule is not strictly followed; thus in Sagittarius (the Archer) the two brightest stars are not Alpha and Beta, but Epsilon and Sigma.

4 False. From Gibraltar the Cross is always well below the horizon.

5 False; Vega is steely blue in colour. The only single naked-eye star which is said to have a greenish tint is Beta Libræ, but most people will certainly call it white, and I admit that I have never seen any colour in it.

6 False. Virgo, the Virgin, represents Astræa, the goddess of justice – daughter of Jupiter and Themis.

7 True.

8 False. The two brightest stars in Orion are Rigel and Betelgeux. Procyon is in the constellation of Canis Minor (the Little Dog).

9 False; there is only one first-magnitude star – Antares, though it is true that two others are above the second magnitude: Lambda Scorpii (1.6) and Theta Scorpii (1.9).

10 True. Cancer lies between the Twins in Gemini to the one side, and the main pattern of Leo on the other. It also borders on Ursa Major and Hydra.

QUIZ 10

1 A star which is made up of two components, moving round their common centre of gravity. They may be virtually equal in size, mass and luminosity, or they may be very unequal and in different stages of evolution, though presumably they have a common origin.

2 A diagram in which the stars are plotted according to their spectral types and their real luminosities. Diagrams of this sort were produced as a result of the

independent work of E. J. Hertzsprung and H. N. Russell.

3 Because it has the greatest proper motion of any known star, amounting to 10.31 seconds of arc per year; in 180 years it crosses the sky by a distance equal to the apparent diameter of the full moon.

4 (a) Cepheid. (b) Long-period or Mira star. (c) Long-period or Mira star. (d) Algol-type eclipsing binary. (e) Cepheid.

5 The apparent magnitude which a star would have if it could be seen from a standard distance of 10 parsecs (32.6 light-years). Thus from this distance Sirius would shine as a star of magnitude 1.4, but Deneb would be −7.5!

6 The letters O B A F G K M R N S are given to the spectral types of stars, in order of decreasing surface temperature, though the surface temperatures of R, N and S stars are about equal at 4500 to 4600°F (2500 to 2600°C).

7 In Aquila. It can still be seen with very powerful telescopes, but has become extremely faint. Its official designation was V.603 Aquilæ. At its peak it reached magnitude −1.1, and is the brightest nova so far seen during the present century.

8 A Type I supernova originates in a binary system, in which one component is a white dwarf. The white dwarf pulls material away from its larger, less dense companion until it becomes unstable, and blows itself to pieces in a matter of seconds, so that it shines temporarily with many millions of times the luminosity of the Sun. A Type II supernova is produced when a

massive star runs out of nuclear 'fuel' and collapses under the influence of gravity; there is an 'implosion', followed by a rebound and a shock-wave which blows most of the star's material away into space, leaving a small, super-dense core made up of neutrons. The last naked-eye supernova was that of 1987, in the Large Cloud of Magellan.

9 (a) A star of spectral type W, with a surface temperature up to 144,000°F (80,000°C). Wolf-Rayet stars are very luminous, and have expanding shells; they are relatively rare. (b) A Brown Dwarf is a star whose mass is so low that nuclear reactions have never been triggered off, so that the star shines feebly because of gravitational contraction. Brown dwarfs must presumably exist, and have been reported from time to time, but it must be admitted that as yet we have no certain observation of any. (c) A variable star, made up of a binary system, which suffers minor outbursts with reasonable regularity; thus RU Pegasi flares up by about three magnitudes every 70 days or so. The best known members of the class are the first discovered (U Geminorum) and the brightest (SS Cygni), so that dwarf novæ are usually termed either SS Cygni or U Geminorum stars.

10 Because these two stars are the closest stars which are reasonably like the Sun, and which might therefore be reasonably expected to be the centres of planetary systems. Both are considerably less luminous than the Sun; their distances are 10.7 light-years (Epsilon Eridani) and 11.9 light-years (Tau Ceti). Not surprisingly, the results of the 1960 experiment were negative.

True or False?

1 False. The number of stars visible with the naked eye is approximately 5800. This means that it is seldom possible to see more than about 2900 stars with the naked eye at any one time (since faint stars near the horizon are bound to be lost). 2500 is a more reasonable figure.

2 False. The proper motion of Hamal is less than 0.2 seconds of arc per year.

3 True. Eta Carinæ, in the far south of the sky, is an erratic variable; in 1840 it was one of the three brightest stars in the sky, but for a century now it has been just below naked-eye visibility.

4 False. At present Sirius is approaching us at 5 miles (8 kilometres) per second, but this will not continue indefinitely, as both Sirius and the Sun are in orbit round the centre of the Galaxy.

5 False. Algol's variations were indeed explained by John Goodricke in 1783; but though Goodricke was deaf and dumb, he was not blind.

6 True. We have no really detailed accounts of it, but it seems to have reached about magnitude −9.5, and remained visible with the naked eye for two years.

7 False. A-type stars are pure white.

8 True; the discovery was made from the equipment on IRAS, the Infra-Red Astronomical Satellite.

9 False. The white dwarf companion of Sirius (Sirius B) was discovered by A. Clark in 1861. However, Adams at Mount Wilson in 1915 showed that instead of being large, red and cool, as had been believed, it

had a very hot surface. This was the first known white dwarf.

10 True. All the other stars within a range of ten light-years are very dim dwarfs, below naked-eye visibility. Within thirteen light-years there are five more naked-eye stars: Epsilon Eridani, 61 Cygni, Epsilon Indi, Procyon and Tau Ceti.

QUIZ 11

1 A galaxy is a star-system, often containing a hundred thousand million stars. A globular cluster is a symmetrical cluster of stars, sometimes more than a million in number, but nothing more than a relatively minor feature of a galaxy.

2 The Seven Sisters – because people with average sight, under good conditions, can see seven individual stars in the cluster. (Keen-sighted people can see more; the record is said to be nineteen.)

3 Præsepe is an open cluster in Cancer, easily visible with the naked eye.

4 M.57: the Ring Nebula. M.97: the Owl Nebula. M.27: the Dumb-bell Nebula. M.8: the Lagoon Nebula. M.45: the Pleiades.

5 It is a dark nebula in the Southern Cross.

6 The Crab Nebula. It lies near the star Zeta Tauri, and can be seen as a faint blur with good binoculars. Photographs taken with powerful telescopes show a highly complicated mass of expanding gas, inside

which is a pulsar – the actual remnant of the
disrupted star.

7 In Orion, not far from Alnitak (Zeta Orionis) in the
Belt. It is a dark nebula, deriving its nickname from its
resemblance to the head of a knight in chess. It is not
difficult to photograph, but is remarkably elusive
visually.

8 Omega Centauri, which is a globular cluster; the
others are open clusters.

9 Harlow Shapley, in 1918. He did so by studying the
short-period variables in globular clusters; these
clusters lie round the edge of the main Galaxy, and
from them he was able to obtain a reasonably good
idea of the dimensions of the Galaxy itself.

10 (c) is correct. The distance between the Sun and
the galactic centre is still rather uncertain; estimates
range between 27,000 and 33,000 light-years, so that
30,000 is a reasonable approximation.

True or False?

1 False. The Milky Way is made up of millions of stars,
together with various other features such as nebulæ
and a tremendous amount of thinly spread interstellar
material.

2 True. Halley discovered it in 1714. It is rather
surprising that there are no earlier reports of it,
because it can just be seen with the naked eye under
good conditions.

3 True. A pulsar is a supernova remnant made up of neutrons. As it spins, it sends out 'pulsed' radio waves, which accounts for its name.

4 True. Jansky was not searching for extraterrestrial radio waves; he was using an improvised aerial to study 'static' on behalf of the Bell Telephone Company, and his discovery of radio waves from the Milky Way was quite unexpected.

5 True. A planetary nebula represents a late stage in the evolution of a star, when it throws off its outer layers – which simply expand into space until they cease to shine.

6 False; the average distances between the stars near the centre of a globular cluster are much more than this. It is not easy to be precise, but the mean figure is probably about a quarter of a light-day, roughly 4000 million miles or almost 6500 million kilometres.

7 True, though some recent estimates make the full diameter of the Galaxy somewhat less than this value.

8 False. The v-formation of the Hyades extends not from Arcturus, but from Aldebaran. (Aldebaran is not a true member of the cluster; it simply happens to lie more or less between the Hyades and ourselves.)

9 False. The centre of the Galaxy lies in the direction of the star-clouds not in Cygnus, but in Sagittarius. We cannot see through to the actual centre, because there is too much 'dust' in the way.

10 False; it would 'weigh' much more than this. The density of neutron star material is estimated to be of the order of a hundred million million times that of water!

QUIZ 12

1 M.31, the Andromeda Spiral, at a distance of 2.2 million light-years. Note that I said 'easily visible', because very keen-sighted people claim to be able to glimpse the slightly more distant Triangulum Spiral, M.33, which is easy enough through binoculars.

2 The Magellanic Clouds, or Nubeculæ, which may be regarded as satellites of our Galaxy, and lie within 200,000 light-years. Both are prominent naked-eye objects, looking superficially rather like detached portions of the Milky Way.

3 Edwin Hubble, in 1923. Using the Mount Wilson reflector, then much the most powerful in the world, Hubble was able to detect Cepheid variables in some of the spirals, notably M.31. Since these Cepheids 'give away' their luminosities by the way in which they fluctuate, Hubble was able to estimate their distances, and it was at once clear that they were much too remote to be members of our Galaxy.

4 The Sword of Orion, which is a gaseous nebula. The others are galaxies.

5 NGC stands for New General Catalogue. This was a catalogue of clusters and nebulæ drawn up in 1888 by the Danish astronomer J. L. E. Dreyer.

6 (c) is correct. The most remote quasars and galaxies are certainly further away then 10,000 million light-years; probably the present limit is around 14,000 million light-years.

7 Because they are so luminous that they can be seen over vast distances, and it is reasonable to assume that supernovæ in external galaxies are about as luminous

as supernovæ in our own Galaxy. They can therefore be used as 'standard candles' in the same way as Cepheids, though they are much less reliable.

8 A Seyfert galaxy is a galaxy with a bright, sometimes almost stellar nucleus and weak spiral arms. Most are thought to be highly active, and many are radio sources. They are so named because attention was first drawn to them in 1943 by Carl Seyfert.

9 Quasars, which are external objects; pulsars are members of our Galaxy (though they have also been identified in the Large Cloud of Magellan).

10 A group of galaxies of which our own Milky Way system is a member. There are three spirals (our Galaxy, M.31 in Andromeda and M.33 in Triangulum), the two Magellanic Clouds, and more than two dozen dwarf systems. There is also Maffei 1, detected by the Italian astronomer Paolo Maffei in 1968, which seems to be a giant elliptical system. If it is about 3,000,000 light-years away it must belong to the Local Group, but it lies near the plane of the Milky Way, and is so heavily obscured that little is known about it.

True or False?

1 False. Every group of galaxies is receding from every other group; but the members of our own Local Group are not receding from our Galaxy.

2 True. The age of the universe, in its present form, seems to be somewhere between 15,000 million and 20,000 million years; most authorities have a preference for the lower value.

3 True. Its magnitude is 12.8, so that a fairly small telescope will show it. It had been photographed frequently before being identified as a quasar in 1962–3, but had always been mistaken for a star.

4 True. M.87 is a giant elliptical in the Virgo cluster of galaxies, and is an exceptionally massive system.

5 False. Many larger galaxies are known – including even the Andromeda Spiral.

6 False. A BL Lacertæ object is not a star, though BL Lacertæ itself was formerly mistaken for one. These objects have almost featureless spectra, but seem to be related to quasars, though they are less luminous; probably they too are the nuclei of very active galaxies. At any rate, they lie far beyond our Galaxy, or even the Local Group.

7 True. The Tarantula is a huge gaseous nebula in the Large Cloud of Magellan, and is the largest known. If it lay as close to us as the Orion Nebula, it would cast shadows.

8 False. From the distance of the Andromeda Spiral, our Galaxy would be a very difficult naked-eye object, assuming that beings there have sight comparable with ours. The Sun, a dwarf star, would be excessively faint, and impossible to pick out from the background blur.

9 False. The Mira stars have no Cepheid-type period-luminosity law, so that they are of no use as 'standard candles'.

10 False. The Whirlpool Galaxy does indeed lie close to Alkaid, but it is just over the boundary of the neighbouring constellation, Canes Venatici (the Hunting Dogs).

QUIZ 13

1 Giotto – named after the Florentine painter Giotto di Bondone, who used the comet as a model for the Star of Bethlehem in his picture 'The Adoration of the Magi'.

2 Pluto: 248 years (to be precise, 247.7 years).

3 Ganymede, Mercury, Io, the Moon, Dione, Juno, Leda.

4 Because the Earth's atmosphere bends or refracts some of the sunlight on to the eclipsed Moon. The Moon becomes dim, and often turns a beautiful coppery colour. There have been reported instances when the Moon has vanished completely, but this is very rare; the visibility depends upon conditions in the Earth's atmosphere.

5 A period of 18 years, 11.3 days, after which the Earth, Sun and Moon return to almost the same relative positions. The Saros can be used to predict eclipses; it is usual for an eclipse to be followed by another eclipse 18 years, 11.3 days later, though the slight differences from one Saros to another mean that the eclipses are not identical. For example, the solar eclipse of 1927 was total over part of England, but the 'return' eclipse of 1945 was not.

6 In New South Wales, in Australia; in the Warrumbungle range.

7 The Counterglow.

8 The spectral series – O B A F G K M R N S – was once believed to represent an evolutionary sequence, with stars of types O and B being the youngest and S

the oldest. This is not true, but we still call O to A stars 'early' and the orange or red stars of types M, R, N and S 'late'.

9 Sigma Octantis. It lies within one degree of the south celestial pole, but is only of magnitude 5.5.

10 Musca. All these constellations were added to the sky at various times, but the rest have been officially rejected.

True or False?

1 False. There are only three: the two Magellanic Clouds, and the Andromeda Spiral. It is, admittedly, claimed that keen-eyed people can glimpse a fourth, the Triangulum Spiral.

2 False. The astronomical unit is the distance between the Earth and the Sun: in round numbers 93,000,000 miles or 150,000,000 kilometres.

3 True. Surprisingly, line-of-sight doubles are very much in the minority.

4 False. It is so named because it was discovered by the American astronomer Lewis Swift. (In fact Swift discovered several comets during his long career.)

5 False. The Moon has nothing whatsoever to do with the seasons.

6 True. At all other times it is drowned by the brightness of the sky.

7 True. The crater will be drawn out into an ellipse because of the effects of foreshortening. Even craters well away from the limb are foreshortened; thus Plato,

the great dark-floored walled plain, is almost perfectly circular, but from Earth looks elliptical.

8 True, because the atmosphere of Venus acts as a 'greenhouse' and raises the temperature above that of airless Mercury – even though Mercury is considerably closer to the Sun.

9 False. Auroræ are very rare from low latitudes, but they can be seen occasionally, and in 1909 an aurora was seen from Singapore, which is within two degrees of the equator.

10 True. The interval between successive new moons is $29\frac{1}{2}$ days, and there are only 28 days in February – 29 in leap years – so that there may be no full moon or no new moon during the month.

QUIZ 14

1 Aurora Australis.

2 (a) Ceres, diameter 623 miles (1003 kilometres) – although this is bound to be rather uncertain; at any rate, Ceres is very much the largest of the asteroids. (b) Vesta, which is the only asteroid ever visible with the naked eye. (c) Chiron, discovered in 1977. (d) Hermes – a real midget, which has now been lost. (e) Icarus and Phæthon.

3 Perihelion: the closest approach of a body to the Sun.
   Perigee: the closest approach of a body to the Earth.
   Quadrature: When the Moon or a planet is at right angles to the Sun as seen from the Earth, it is at quadrature. The Moon is at quadrature when half-phase.

Opposition: When a planet is exactly opposite the Sun in the sky it is said to be at opposition, and is best placed for observation.

Inferior conjunction: The position of a planet (or other body) when approximately between the Sun and the Earth. Of the planets, only Mercury and Venus can pass through inferior conjunction. If the alignment is perfect, we have a transit of the body concerned.

Aphelion: the furthest distance of a body from the Sun.

4 Aristarchus, which can often be seen clearly even when on the night side of the Moon.

5 8.6 minutes.

6 La Palma (not Las Palmas, please note!).

7 Via Lactea is the old Latin name for the Milky Way.

8 Arcturus: K. Vega: A. Betelgeux: M. Antares: M. Pollux: K. Sirius: A.

9 Both are interstellar clouds, consisting largely of hydrogen, but in an H.II region the hydrogen is ionized by very hot stars in suitable positions, and emits light. Emission nebulæ such as the Sword of Orion are therefore H.II regions.

10 Twinkling is due to the effects of the Earth's atmosphere. A star is virtually a point source, and twinkles obviously even when high up; the lower the star, the greater the layer of atmosphere through which its light has to pass, and the greater the twinkling. A planet appears as a tiny disk rather than a point source, and so the twinkling is less. Twinkling is known officially as 'scintillation'.

111

True or False?

1 False. Only a little over a hundred globulars are known in our Galaxy.

2 True – though his English is so perfect that you would never realize that it is not his native language unless he told you!

3 True. It is the far-southern Mensa, the Table (originally Mons Mensæ, the Table Mountain). It does, however, contain a large part of the Large Cloud of Magellan.

4 False. The Pole Star does not revolve round the Sun. However, precession effects mean that the north celestial pole describes a circle in the sky in a period of about 26,000 years.

5 False. His name was Konstantin Eduardovich Tsiolkovskii (alternatively spelled Tsiolkovsky, Tsiolkovskiy or even Ziolkovsky). Tchaikovsky was the great Russian composer.

6 False. The Earth's orbit round the Sun is absolutely stable.

7 False. The Turkish flag shows the crescent Moon together with a star, but there is no evidence that the 'star' represents Venus.

8 False. Europa has an icy, smooth surface. It is the inner large satellite, Io, which has a red, sulphury surface and highly active volcanoes.

9 True. Wolf Creek, 2788 feet (850 metres) in diameter, is undoubtedly meteoritic. With the exception of the Arizona structure, it is probably the best preserved of all terrestrial impact craters.

10 False. Phœbe is the name of the outermost satellite of Saturn.

QUIZ 15

1 Ole Rømer, in 1675.

2 Jupiter.

3 *Viking 1* landed in Chryse, and *Viking 2* in Utopia.

4 A period between 1645 and 1715 when, from all the available evidence, there were practically no sunspots, so that the solar cycle was suspended. The cause of this is not known, but so far as we can tell there have also been earlier spotless periods. The name is due to E. W. Maunder, who was one of the first to draw attention to it.

5 Lunar Orbiters. All five were completely successful.

6 Professor Sir Francis Graham-Smith.

7 It is on the western limb, though Mare Orientale means 'Eastern Sea'. In fact I discovered and named it, long before the Space Age, but a subsequent edict by the International Astronomical Union reversed east and west on the Moon. (I opposed the change, but I was heavily outvoted!)

8 Altair, which is a white star. All the others are red or orange-red.

9 Pegasus, the Flying Horse.

10 Texas.

True or False?

1 True. The Triangulum Spiral is a galaxy, whereas the Solar System is a very minor part of our own Galaxy.

2 False. Phœbe is the only satellite of Saturn to have retrograde motion; all the rest, including Hyperion, have direct motion. It is probable that Phœbe is a captured asteroid rather than a genuine satellite.

3 False. It lies in the constellation of Octans.

4 False. Arcturus, about 115 times as luminous as the Sun, is very feeble compared with 'searchlights' such as Rigel (60,000 Sun-power). Some stars are known to have more than a million times the Sun's luminosity.

5 False. The first American in space was Alan Shepard, in 1961. Glenn was, however, the first American to complete one full orbit round the Earth, in 1962.

6 True. He was appointed Director in 1675, when the Observatory was founded, and remained so until his death in 1720. He was also the first Astronomer Royal, though during his first few years at Greenwich the title was unofficial.

7 False. There can never be more than seven eclipses in any one year; thus in 1935 there were five solar and two lunar eclipses, and in 1984 there were four solar and three lunar.

8 False. Toro, Asteroid No. 1685, moves round the Sun in the same way as any other asteroid. Its period is 1.6 years, and its distance from the Sun ranges between 0.8 and 1.96 astronomical units. (When it was

discovered, in 1948, Press reports indicated that it was a minor Earth satellite, but this is quite wrong.)

9 True. The KAO or Kulper Airborne Observatory has been most successful.

10 False. Herschel did indeed take a large telescope to the southern hemisphere for this purpose, but he went to Feldhausen, at the Cape in South Africa, not to New South Wales.

QUIZ 16

1 Biela's Comet used to have a period of 6.6 years. At the return of 1845 it split in two. The twins returned in 1852, but have never been seen since, and the comet has certainly disintegrated. For some years meteors (the Bielids) were seen coming from the position where the comet ought to have been, but the shower has now become so feeble that it cannot usually be identified.

2 Two: Triton and Nereid. A third satellite has been suspected, but not confirmed.

3 On Io, Jupiter's innermost large satellite; they are active volcanoes.

4 Prominences, rising from the surface of the Sun. They are not flames, but masses of glowing hydrogen. With the naked eye they can be seen only during a total solar eclipse, though instruments based upon the principle of the spectroscope mean that they can be examined at any time.

5 For his invention of the Schmidt telescope (or Schmidt camera), which uses a spherical mirror and a specially shaped correcting plate. It means that large

areas of the sky can be photographed successfully with a single exposure.

6 One million.

7 It is the recurrent nova T Coronæ, in Corona Borealis (the Northern Crown). Its usual magnitude is about 10, but twice, in 1866 and 1946, it has flared up briefly to naked-eye visibility.

8 In Vela (the Sails) and Carina (the Keel); the four stars are Iota and Epsilon Carinæ, and Kappa and Delta Velorum. The arrangement is very like that of the Southern Cross but the False Cross is larger, and its stars are not so bright as the three leaders of the Southern Cross. It is too far south to be seen from anywhere in Europe.

9 (a) Menkar. (b) Bellatrix. (c) Mizar. (d) Achernar. (e) Spica.

10 (c) is correct; the Observatory lies near Leningrad.

True or False?

1 False. Pulsars, or neutron stars, are minor features of galaxies.

2 True. Since Alpha Centauri is only about 4.3 light-years away, the constellation patterns would not be very different from those we see, and the Sun would indeed be in Cassiopeia.

3 False. Mira Ceti is the famous long-period variable Omicron Ceti.

4 True. It made three active passes of Mercury, in March and September 1974 and March 1975. Contact with it was finally lost on 24 March 1975, though no

doubt the probe is still in solar orbit and still making periodical approaches to Mercury.

5 False: NASA stands for National Aeronautics and Space Administration.

6 False. On the outward journey *Apollo 13* was crippled by an on-board explosion, and no lunar landing was achieved, though the astronauts returned safely.

7 True. Helium was identified in the solar spectrum by Sir Norman Lockyer in 1868; not until 1894 was it detected on Earth, by Sir William Ramsay, as a gas occluded in cleveite.

8 False. Neptune is slightly smaller than Uranus, though appreciably more massive.

9 True. In ancient times it was thought that the 'evening star', Hesperus, and the 'morning star', Phosphorus, were different bodies, though at a fairly early stage it was realized that they are the same – Venus.

10 True. Earlier probes to Venus had been launched, but without obtaining any useful results.

QUIZ 17

1 Barwell.

2 Only one: Ganymede, in Jupiter's system. Both Callisto in Jupiter's system and Titan in Saturn's system are now known to be slightly smaller. The diameter of Triton, the major satellite of Neptune, is not yet known with precision, but is almost certainly less than that of Mercury.

3 When the planet Venus passes in transit on to the face of the Sun, it seems to draw a strip of blackness after it, and when this strip disappears the transit has already begun (when the trailing edge of the planet passes the Sun's limb) – so that it is impossible to time the moment of immersion accurately. This 'Black Drop' effect ruined the method of measuring the distance of Venus, and hence of the Sun, by transit observations. It is due to the fact that Venus is surrounded by a dense atmosphere.

4 (a) The Sea of Clouds. (b) The Bay of Heats. (c) The Marsh of Clouds. (d) The Central Bay. (e) Humboldt's Sea.

5 Percival Lowell, mainly to carry out his studies of Mars. It is today one of the world's major observatories.

6 (c) is correct. The name comes from Ares, which is the Greek equivalent of the war-god Mars.

7 Chi Cygni: long-period (Mira star). Beta Doradûs: Cepheid. R Hydræ: long-period (Mira star). Beta Pegasi: semi-regular variable. Lambda Tauri: Algol-type eclipsing binary.

8 Vulpecula (the Fox) was originally known as Vulpecula et Anser (the Fox and Goose). The Goose disappeared long ago (I have suggested that the fox must have eaten it).

9 Receding.

10 Venus, Mars, Jupiter, Sirius, Capella. (Only on rare occasions can Mars outshine Jupiter. The maximum magnitude of Jupiter is -2.6, and of Mars -2.8.)

True or False?

1 False. Few open clusters contain more than a few hundreds of stars, whereas a globular cluster may contain more than a million.

2 False. Both M.97 (the Owl) and M.27 (the Dumb-bell) are planetary nebulæ in our Galaxy.

3 False, though it used to be true. Precession has now shifted the vernal equinox, or First Point of Aries, out of Aries (the Ram) into the adjacent constellation of Pisces (the Fishes).

4 True. The magnitude of Spica is 0.98, and of Deneb 1.25. Admittedly Deneb is much the more luminous, but it is also much further away.

5 True. The barycentre is the centre of gravity of the Earth–Moon system; because the Moon has only $\frac{1}{81}$ the mass of the Earth, the barycentre lies deep within the Earth's globe.

6 True; it is the 236-inch (600-centimetre) reflector at Zelenchukskaya.

7 True. Both are lunar craters. Barrow is named after Isaac Barrow, colleague of Isaac Newton, and Birmingham after the nineteenth-century Irish astronomer John Birmingham.

8 False. It was Halley's Comet which was seen a few months before the Battle of Hastings. The nearest English total eclipse to the Battle of Hastings was that of 1140.

9 False, though until the pass of *Mariner 4* in 1965 it was generally believed to be true. We now know that not all the dark areas are depressions – some are

119

plateaux – and the darkness is not due to any organic material.

10 True. It was very small, but it worked, and it must be regarded as the true ancestor of the spacecraft of today.

QUIZ 18

1 (b) is correct. Snickers is the nickname often given to a very small dwarf galaxy in our Local Group.

2 1 January, 2001 (not 1 January 2000, as so many people think; the year 2000 is the last year of the twentieth century).

3 He didn't! Possibly he suggested the experiment, but there is no evidence that he ever carried it out, though some later scientists may have done so.

4 Nowhere, because Vulcan does not exist. During the nineteenth century it was often thought that unexplained irregularities in the movements of Mercury indicated the presence of an inter-Mercurial planet, and the French astronomer Le Verrier, for one, was convinced of its existence; it was named Vulcan. However, the movements of Mercury have now been thoroughly explained by relativity theory, and there is no doubt that Vulcan is a myth.

5 (d) is correct. An ocular is merely another name for an eyepiece.

6 None. There is no such thing as an annular eclipse of the Moon.

7 The dwarf kept by the eccentric Danish astronomer, Tycho Brahe, at the observatory on the Baltic island of Hven, used by Tycho from 1576 to 1596.

8 (d) is correct. Polyhymnia is asteroid No. 33, discovered in 1854. It has a revolution period of 4.8 years, and is about 28 miles (45 kilometres) in diameter. It never becomes much brighter than the eleventh magnitude.

9 Bees. The patterns had been incorporated in the columns outside the main doors of the building, but when seen by one of the trustees were regarded as undignified; moreover, the bee was apparently about to sting a man on the nose – and this was taken to represent Charles T. Yerkes, the millionaire who had financed the Observatory, being stung for the money!

10 W. T. Hay, otherwise known as Will Hay. He was an enthusiastic and skilful amateur observer.

True or False?

1 False. An achondrite is a type of stony meteorite.

2 False. If a source of light is receding, all the lines in its spectrum are shifted over to the red or long-wave end of the spectral band; this is known as the Red Shift. The greater the Red Shift, the greater the velocity of recession.

3 True.

4 False. The name is in honour of an Australian astronomer, the late Colin Gum.

5 False. Forbidden lines are spectral lines which do not show up under normal terrestrial conditions, but can

be seen in the spectra of some celestial objects, where conditions are very different.

6 True. John Flamsteed, the first Astronomer Royal, was installed at Greenwich to prepare a new star catalogue, but he was slow in publishing his results, and eventually his colleagues, Newton and Halley, lost patience and published them without Flamsteed's authorization. The furious Flamsteed managed to obtain some of the copies, and burned them in public.

7 False. Ra-Shalom is an Aten-type asteroid with a revolution period of 283 days, so that its orbit is smaller than that of the Earth. Its distance from the Sun ranges between 43,000,000 miles (69,000,000 kilometres) and 79,000,000 miles (127,000,000 kilometres).

8 False – just! Parts of the mounting for the aerial were indeed made from the parts of a dismantled car; but it was a Ford, not a Morris.

9 False. No further comment is needed!

10 True. The automatic transit instrument at La Palma was financed by the Carlsberg company, and is therefore known as the Carlsberg Transit Instrument.

QUIZ 19

1 (a) is correct.

2 Because Stickney was the maiden name of the wife of the discoverer of the two Martian satellites, Asaph Hall. Following an unsuccessful search for satellites in

1877, Mrs Hall persuaded her husband to persist for just one more night – and he did so, with success.

3 Hellas and Argyre.

4 Arion. According to the story, Arion was a famous singer who always won every competition for which he entered. When returning by ship from one competition, together with his prizes, the sailors threw him overboard, but he was rescued by a kindly dolphin and brought safely to the shore. When the dolphin died, at an advanced age, it was rewarded with a place in the sky.

5 R Aræ, which is an Algol-type eclipsing binary. All the others are long-period variables (Mira stars).

6 Andriyan Nikolayev and Pavel Popovich.

7 A law of sunspot distribution. At the start of a new cycle, spots appear in high latitudes, 30 to 40 degrees north or south of the solar equator. As the cycle progresses, the spots appear at lower and lower latitudes, and may be seen to within five degrees of the equator; as spots of the old cycle die out, the first spots of the new cycle appear in the high latitudes. This phenomenon was first studied in detail by Gustav Spörer, though it seems to have been discovered earlier by the English amateur R. C. Carrington around 1865.

8 (c) is correct. The stars in Aquila above magnitude 3.5 are Alpha or Altair (0.8), Gamma (2.7), Zeta (3.0), Theta (3.2), and Delta and Lambda (each 3.4).

9 Beta Carinæ: Miaplacidus. Theta Eridani: Acamar. Eta Virginis: Zaniah. Sigma Sagittarii: Nunki. Alpha Crateris: Alkes.

10 The relationship between the distance of a galaxy and its velocity of recession; 'the further, the faster'. The precise value of the Hubble Constant is still uncertain. Estimates range between 40 and 100 kilometres per second per megaparsec, but the favoured value is around 55 kilometres per second per megaparsec.

True or False?

1 False. Declination is the angular distance of a body north or south of the celestial equator; celestial latitude is the angular distance north or south of the ecliptic.

2 False. It was a globe 7.3 feet (4 metres) in diameter made by H. Busch in Denmark around 1654–64. It was a crude ancestor of the modern planetarium; the audience sat inside it, and looked at the artificial stars painted on the inside of the globe.

3 False. The planets always referred to as the inferior planets are Mercury and Venus, which are closer to the Sun than we are.

4 False insofar as W. C. Bond is concerned; despite his initials (standing for William Cranch) there is no evidence that he had any connection with lavatories, flush or otherwise! However, James Nasmyth, the famous observer of the Moon, did invent the steam-hammer.

5 True. In 1856 the Director of the Armagh Observatory, the rather ferocious Dr Romney Robinson, petitioned the House 'against the Newry-Enniskillen railway'. He was successful, and this resulted in an Act prohibiting 'the transit of locomotive engines or

carriages' within 700 yards of the observatory without the consent of the Director, which, of course, would on no account be given! When, in 1858, the Newry Railway Company gave notice of a Bill authorizing them to make a branch to a terminus near Dean's Bridge, in Armagh, Robinson made a firm entry in his notebook: 'It will not come within the limit, I believe, but I shall watch them carefully.'

6 False. A Julian day is measured by a count of the days, starting from 12 noon on 1 January, 4713 BC. The system was devised in 1582 by the mathematician Scaliger, who named it in honour of his father, Julius Scaliger; it has nothing to do with Julius Cæsar.

7 True.

8 True. All these are craters on Mercury.

9 True.

10 False. It was discovered by J. D. Titius, but Bode popularized it.

QUIZ 20

1 (a) On Saturn's satellite Mimas. (b) On Saturn's satellite Rhea. (c) On Saturn's satellite Iapetus. (d) On Jupiter's satellite Europa. (e) On Jupiter's satellite Callisto.

2 Edmund Neison Nevill, who wrote under his name of Neison. He went to Natal in 1882, to establish the observatory and make studies of the transit of Venus, and remained as director until the observatory was

closed down in 1911 because of lack of money. Nothing of it now remains.

3 M.87: in Virgo. M.81: Ursa Major. M.67: Cancer. M.32: Andromeda. M.102: Nowhere – it was one of the missing numbers in Messier's catalogue. It may possibly have been identical with M.101, a spiral galaxy in Ursa Major, but may well have been a comet which – for once – Messier failed to recognize.

4 The Old Royal Observatory at Greenwich. When King Charles II decided to found the Observatory, he commissioned Christopher Wren to design the first buildings, and paid for them by selling old and decayed gunpowder to the French.

5 Alphonsus, which is in the lunar highlands south of Ptolemæus. All the other craters in the list are in the Mare Imbrium.

6 The star names are Svalocin (Alpha Delphini) and Rotanev (Beta Delphini). They were named by Nicolaus Venator, and the names are reversals of his own name.

7 Crommelin's Comet, because it was A. C. D. Crommelin who showed the identity of the comets discovered at various returns by Pons, Coggia, Winnecke and Forbes. The comet has a period of just over 27 years, and was last at perihelion in 1985.

8 (a) Eros. (b) Wilhelm Beer, who collaborated with Johann von Mädler in their great book about the Moon published in 1838. (c) Peenemünde, where the team headed by Wernher von Braun was engaged in building V.2 rockets. (d) Herschel. (e) James Bradley.

9 It is the largest tektite ever found; it weighs 3.2 kilograms.

10 Alcor; it is the naked-eye companion of Mizar (Zeta Ursæ Majoris) in the Plough.

True or False?

1 True. He was Urbain Le Verrier – it was said of him that although he may not have been the most detestable man in France, he was certainly the most destested! However, he was reinstated when his successor, Delaunay, was drowned in a boating accident.

2 False. One sol is a Martian day (approximately $24\frac{1}{2}$ hours). Phobos has a revolution period of only $7\frac{1}{2}$ hours, which is less than a sol, but the revolution period of Deimos is 30 hours, which is more than a sol.

3 False. These effects are *librations*, not liberations!

4 False. It is the limit of the area in which the Sun's influence is dominant, beyond which the solar wind ceases to be detectable. No man-made probe has yet reached it.

5 False. The Einstein Observatory can never be visited by anybody; it was an x-ray artificial satellite, 20.9 feet (6.4 metres) long, and was put into an orbit at a height of 500 miles (800 kilometres). It operated from November 1978 to early 1981, and was very successful. Contact with it has now been lost.

6 False. In 1800 a group of astronomers met at the observatory of Johann Schröter, near Lilienthal in Germany, and formed an association to search for a new planet between the orbits of Mars and Jupiter. They called themselves the Celestial Police, and set to work. In 1801 Piazzi at Palermo (not then a member of

127

the group) discovered the first asteroid, Ceres; between 1802 and 1809 the members of the Police discovered three more (Pallas, Juno and Vesta). No more seemed to be forthcoming, and the Police disbanded. The next asteroid was not found until 1845.

7 False. No South American terrorist of this name is known.

8 False. Ursa Major covers 1280 square degrees; Virgo is slightly larger, covering 1294 square degrees.

9 True.

10 False. The members of the Hirayama family are asteroids.

List of Illustrations